Won't He Do It...
YES HE WILL!

Joyce R. Rogers

Won't He Do It… YES HE WILL!

Copyright © 2020 Joyce R. Rogers

Inspired 4 U Publications
Publisher@inspired4uministries.com
www.howtoselfpublishinexcellence.com

ISBN-13: 978-0-9994252-4-4

CONTENTS

"11 For I know the thoughts that I think toward you, saith the LORD, thoughts of peace, and not of evil, to give you an expected end."

(Jeremiah 29:11)

ACKNOWLEDGMENTS

Giving all honor to my God, the Great I Am! All those of African descent, all Africans residing in Niger, Africa, in particular, as my African Ancestry DNA results informed me I am descendent of YOU! To Mary Elizabeth Green, my great-grandmother, whom I love and miss so much, I'm honored to have known you. To Elsie Brooks, my grandmother, whom I never had the honor of meeting before your departure from earth, I wish I could have known you. To Rosalie Elizabeth Matthews-Mitchell, my mother, a very special woman from God, what an honor to have traveled through you all to enter planet earth! What an amazing, powerful, and illumined lineage to come through. Thank you all for making the way for me to enter earth; I would not be who I am without all of you! Thanks-A-Million.

To my siblings: Angela M. Langston, who departed this earth too soon, you were one of God's Scribes; Robert C. Littlejohn, your departure from earth really shook my foundation, you were our Enoch; Vanessa Kirby-Foote, God's Herbalist, I would be remiss not to include you, who has been a part of this family forever. Thank you for being a true sister, it means more to me than you know; Charles W. Rogers, thank you for defeating stage four cancer and showing forth God's glory, you are the Joseph of this family; Deborah A. Sturgis, I am so happy you were able to join the family, you fit in like a missing perfect puzzle piece because of the Angel you are, thank you for being so loving and accepting of us, you really are God's Majestic Angel; Gregory A. Rogers, thank you for taking on your battle with cancer and winning, you are God's Weeping Prophet, the world needs you, and you have a lot to give; David S. Mitchell, God's Psalmist, continue destroying the works of the enemy with songs; Michael E. Brown, God's Prophet, continue to come into the knowledge of who you are, and help reform this world; and last but not least Joseph T. Mitchell. To my brother Terrell Simms, you were so handsome. I remember when I tried to flirt with you, and you ran me home because you knew what I didn't know - that you were my brother, and then you were gone. We didn't get the chance to know one another before you departed this earth. You were gone too soon; I'll never understand.

To my children: Shannon Henderson, Aleeta LaShawn Rogers, Eugene Daryl Martin, Charles William Rogers, Kernell Mark Hunt, Jr., Marcus Malcolm Hunt, Sherika Nicole Hunt, Monique Sheree Hunt, and Emmanuel Messiah Hunt, I want you all to know it was an honor parenting you, and having each of you develop your earth suit in my Womb. The bond I have with each of you is something neither of you may ever understand; just know I am truly blessed because of you, so thank you for agreeing to come through me.

To my sons from another mother: Booker T. Wilson, I love you as if you were my own. I am so proud of you, thank you for accepting me in your life I am eternally grateful. To Blair Brown, you have been a long-time welcome member of our family, always a good time when you were around. I love you and thank you for becoming a part of our family. To Ken Wright, you fit perfectly into our family, I am happy to have you as my son, you are a very special young man, remain true to yourself, and you will continue to go far. You know I love you. To Andrew Brown, it is really an honor having you share in our family as one of my sons. I am so proud of you and all that you are accomplishing in your life. Thank you for accepting me; I love you as one of my own. To Wajutome Goodluck Obriko, you are amazing and spoiled, I am so grateful you came into my life when you did, thank you for being you. I love you.

To my grandchildren: Mikira, Mahogany, Malachi, MaKye, Jacob, Kejuan, Prayer, Ta'Shari, Ja'Khari, Eugene, Eehyn, Caiden, Kaiyanna, Keira, Nasir, Armani, Ava, Aubre', Marcus, Jr., Charleigh, Emmanuel, Jr., and Kernell, III., I pray you all someday find it in your hearts to forgive all who came before you for not providing a better world for you to enjoy, and be bold enough to do your part to make this world a better place for those who follow you. I love each one of you more than you will ever know; I am proud you are my grandchildren. Thank you for agreeing to come through this lineage. As I release this Book, my second great-grandchild is going through the process of development in the womb of Ta'Shari who happens to be born in the same month and on the same day as her cousin, the mother of my first great-grandchild, may your Children bring to this earth many answers to assist in the restoration of harmony to this Universe.

To my great-grandchildren: Nataliyah born to MiKira, the first to enter earth, and all the others resting as seeds in the loins of the rest of my grandchildren, awaiting your time of entry into earth, it is my prayer before your conception, the physical, emotional, and financial status of our lineage provides a way for all of you to never have to experience poverty, nor physical or mental illnesses in the way other generations before you have so when you enter this realm, your focus will be on serving the divine purpose for which you have come to planet earth. I love you all to the moon and beyond, may every generation following, and including yours be blessed above measure!

To: Michael O. Takyi, a very special nephew from another lineage, welcome to your new family! To the many nieces, nephews, cousins, and host of relatives and friends in the earth and your seed, may you know the powerful lineage you are blessed to be a part of, it is my hope you will always be committed to bringing the family together in unison. I pray many blessings upon each and every one of you. To God be ALL the Glory for the things He has done, is doing, and shall continue to do through us all!

FOREWORD

This book is for every person who has ever needed God to "do it." Whatever your "it" is, the author, Joyce R. Rogers, takes you on a power-packed journey of her own life and how God did it for her.

I first met Joyce in a personal development workshop hosted by our mutual friend. She commanded my attention, not just because of the bad white pantsuit she was sporting, but there was something about her voice that let everyone in the room know she was a woman of depth and experience. In other words, she knew what she was talking about; so when Joyce spoke, people listened.

It would be a few years later that we were together once again at a glorious resort in Seattle, Washington for a self-care retreat, and once again, Joyce left each woman in the room on bated breath as she would from time to time stand up and declare what the Spirit was speaking to her.

That is why I was so concerned when I heard that my sister Joyce had fallen critically ill upon her return from that retreat. How could she be in the hospital, I thought to myself? How could things be this serious for a woman I had just hugged tightly a few days earlier?

It would be another year until she began to share the full story with me about how a health crisis took her on an unbelievable transformation journey. And even as she shared her story of miracles upon miracles with me, Joyce told me that she knew there was still continued emotional soul work for her to do.

I am beyond grateful for how God allowed me to be a witness to Joyce's continual elevation in life, as well as in the Spirit realm.

This written work is so much more than a book, but it is a testament of what it means to love and live your life. There is so much wisdom from her story of marriage, motherhood, health, and wealth, and it all seems to bring the reader back to the center of yourself and your own life choices. It is an invitation to the better parts of you that are often ignored, pushed to the back of life, or worst yet, left on the side of the road for dead.

But Joyce will share with you a literal resurrection and what it looks like to live out a second chance; and the blessings that await you if you dare to do the same.

I have no doubt that you will be inspired to make some major moves in your own life. It is my prayer that you will let go of hesitation and questioning your readiness for what God has already ordained as yours.

You will see that as long as you are still here, there is a chance to change, and the quality of life is determined by the level you choose to live it.

I am proud to say that Joyce R. Rogers has decided to live her life. Ready or not, she is speaking her truth to the world. Her goal is not popularity, riches, or fame. But her deepest desire is to be faithful to those things that have been divinely given to her. She takes her responsibility of planting in the garden of life seriously, and like her, I can sense that a divine harvest is coming. And if you have an inner knowing that you are meant for so much more, may you be encouraged to not wait until crisis, the pain of brokenness, or a near-death experience to do what you came to this earth to do. More than anything, may you know the time is NOW.

As you read Joyce's story, I hope you will feel her heart, and in turn, ignite a fire in your own. Her story is our story. God did it for her, and I know God will do it for you!

Melissa Brown
The Soul Love Coach

Bless the Lord, O my soul, and forget not all his benefits:
³ Who forgiveth all thine iniquities; who healeth all thy diseases;
⁴ Who redeemeth thy life from destruction; who crowneth thee with
lovingkindness and tender mercies; ⁵ Who satisfieth thy mouth with
good things; so that thy youth is renewed like the eagle's.

(Psalm 103:2-5)

INTRODUCTION

Following is the Author's account of miraculous events in her life she was able to experience to share with the world today. It is the Author's hope to bring God from an abstract concept in the sky to your recognizing Him in the daily activities of your lives. She gives accounts of how she says God brought her back from death after suffering a ruptured Aneurysm, to surviving Leukemia after being diagnosed the very next year of surviving the Aneurysm, to being in her right mind following a divorce after 33 years of being in relationship with her now ex-husband in the midst of her treatment for Leukemia, to losing everything through this process and having to start her life over at the tender age of 58.

While this book is entitled, "Won't He Do It... YES HE WILL!" the Author wants you to know she is not oblivious to the reality that everyone doesn't make it, and that we have lost many of our loved ones to various sicknesses and diseases or senseless other methods of death, and many who yet live are surviving in such conditions of hopelessness wherein they are merely existing in life and not thriving, living paycheck to paycheck or no check at all. It is her sincere desire to restore hope to those individuals, to rekindle their faith in the possibility of a life well-lived.

The Author would like to first give honor to those who have transitioned from this realm, and she prays a special shield of comfort to all who mourn those losses. Secondly, she prays those who are struggling in conditions that seem insurmountable, after reading the many testimonies herein, will become empowered to know there is hope, and their situation really can change for the better.

She notes here when God spoke to her while in the hospital to inform her, she was going to survive cancer (Leukemia), she recalled her first thought being, 'I don't know why some live and some die." She really did not know, but one thing she knew was God was alive and well and is real despite our circumstances. While recovering, she remembered waking up every day, realizing she had lost everything down to the clothes on her back, asking, "How do I begin again?" Therefore, she wants to encourage those, who may be having a hard time identifying with the title of this book, its cover, or anything that may be contained herein to know she understands, and she prays your strength in the Lord.

It is the Author's hope you have the strength to read this book with an open mind, allowing the power of the Holy Spirit to guide you through to the end! She prays there is something written herein to uplift every reader who dares to read this living testament. She believes if you have but a mustard seed of faith and a flicker of a flame of strength to read on, she can assure you the breath of the Living God will fan and ignite your flame, and you will find strength beyond this world to stand up in your truth and be transformed by the renewing of your mind to be able to change the current trajectory of your life and that of your lineage.

She says, "Won't He Do It... YES HE WILL!" is exactly what God has done for her. She shares several accounts of God showing up in her life at a time she so desperately needed Him, noting while some things shared herein may seem unorthodox, they occur more often than not in the lives of everyday people regularly. She says they are simply not acknowledged or shared most of the time. The Author wants you to know these are her accounts of actual events in her life. It is the Author's desire to revive hope in the hearts and minds of the masses to know what God has done for her, He can and will do for all who ask and believe.

"Won't He Do It... YES HE WILL!" is a tangible look at the power of God in operation in the life of one of His chosen vessels today. It gives you an inside look at how God moved in various ways in the life of one Spirit Being living through her earthly experiences. She has shared her first-hand accounts with God showing up and showing out on her behalf in this book. Although the pronoun "He" is used throughout, the Author wants you to know it is simply a point of reference as the true and Living God is both male and female, we are made in His image. The GREAT I Am.

Joyce R. Rogers is an Anointed, Chosen, and Sent Vessel of the Living God, with a strong prophetic voice in the 21st Century as an Ambassador of Christ. She is not afraid to boldly proclaim the power of God at work in the earth today. This book is perfectly timed when there is so much chaos in our world, causing people to lose faith and hope in the true and Living God. Upon reading this book, you will be propelled higher in your faith walk; and those who question if God is real will gain insight and a sense of relief discovering God is not only real but still in the miracle-working business.

The Author proclaims God is alive and well, and believes her life is proof of this fact. This is not just a book but a living testament to the wonder-working power of God in the earth. It is one thing to read about the power of God in the lives of so many in Centuries past, but this book affords a fresh look at some of the miraculous works God is performing in the lives of His people today.

The accounts in this book are awe-inspiring and life-altering. To God be all the Glory for the things He has done and is doing!

DEDICATION

Abba Father,

I surrendered to your power at work in me and birthed this book to encourage all who need to be reminded of who YOU are in their darkest hour. Thank you for having Your way in my life and allowing me to pour my story into the pages of this book as I illustrate how you so gracefully allowed me to be broken so You could show forth your power of restoration.

I pray I have gloried You in the pages of this book, which I dedicate to You, the True and Living God! Thank you for never leaving me nor forsaking me, and for giving me this opportunity to share with the World what You have done for me, knowing you will do for all who diligently seek You!

In YOU, I trust... Forever, Your daughter

"Joyce"

.

"11 Thou hast turned for me my mourning into dancing: thou hast put off my sackcloth, and girded me with gladness;
12 To the end that my glory may sing praise to thee, and not be silent. O LORD my God, I will give thanks unto thee forever."

(Psalm 30:11-12)

SPECIAL THANK YOU

❧⟷❧

To Pastor **Eric Thompson**, who selflessly gave of himself for the editing and financial support of this Book. So how do I say, thank you? What he brought to this work is beyond amazing!

I can say God used him as the icing, topping, and flavoring to assure each reader would experience the power of this work. So thank you, really isn't good enough. Pastor Eric, I love you, and as I've always said, you demonstrate the love of God in ways man isn't accustomed to experiencing in this earth realm, and I know it's because you are totally surrendered to how God wants things done. Thank you, thank you, thank you for being such a yielded vessel for God's use.

Thanks-A-Million

Pastor

❧⟷❧

Now to my Publisher, **JoAnne Meekins** of Inspired 4 U Publications, thank you for your patience, love, and support of this work. I am so proud I came to my senses and allowed you to put your anointed touch on the final work to get it out to the masses. I appreciate you more than you will ever know. I am grateful God allowed our paths to cross, and I am looking forward to where we're going together.

May YOU Be Blessed Above Measure!

Special Thank You!

To the one and only

Melissa Edwards Brown

for prophetically speaking this Book into existence.

Less than four weeks after you spoke the Word of God, the first draft of the Manuscript was completed!

Thanks-A-Million

A Gracious Thank You to my daughter

Monique S. Hunt

Who thought it not robbery to provide, without me asking, the rest of the financing of this Book. Thank you just doesn't suffice, but just know you are a very special young lady, and I am eternally grateful to YOU!

A very Sincere and Unique Thank You to my Ex-husband

Kernell M. Hunt, Sr.

Had it not been for those 33-years with you, good, bad, or indifferent, this Book would not exist! Thank you for your love and financial support of this work.

A very Humble Thank You

Rhonda Bolden

For your incredible Faith and love of the people of God, Thank You for standing in the gap for me, I appreciate you more than you will ever know!

Thanks-A-Million!

Pastor Rhonda

Honorary Thank YOU

Spencer W. Boyer, Sr.

God's Archangel! Pastor, I don't want to imagine where my life would be if God hadn't brought you in when He did, I love you MORE than YOU will ever know!

Thanks-A-Million!

Pastor Boyer

"*7 Though I walk in the midst of trouble, thou wilt revive me: thou shalt stretch forth thine hand against the wrath of mine enemies, and thy right hand shall save me. 8 The LORD will perfect that which concerneth me: thy mercy, O LORD, endureth for ever: forsake not the works of thine own hands.*"

(Psalm 138:7-8)

Chapter 1

ESCAPING DEATH,
SURVIVING A RUPTURED ANEURYSM

On January 24, 2014, I awoke to a beautifully bright sunshiny cold winter morning, which I didn't recognize as being any different from any other morning I arose. Yet it was completely different from any other day of my life as this would be the day I enter my bathroom of my own accord but would later be carried out on a stretcher by paramedics. In what seemed like a matter of seconds after entering my bathroom, I would fall over on the floor dead. I had suffered an Aneurysm. In fact, my blood vessel had burst, and blood was invading parts of the body it was not designed to reach, causing havoc within my anatomy. I've been told by medical professionals had everything I needed not been in place that morning I would not be here. "Won't He Do It… YES HE WILL!"

It started with my husband, who always left the house early in the morning being held back by something intriguing to him on the news, so he was sitting on our bed when he heard my body hit the floor. He tells me my body fell across the entranceway of the bathroom, making it extremely hard for him to enter to find out what was happening, so he called the paramedics as I was nonresponsive.

The reason this is so important is because our bedroom was off the kitchen, and the other bedrooms on that level were on the other side of the house and downstairs, and while some of the children were home, they all were in their bedrooms. I can guarantee you it would have been too late by the time any of the children found me if my husband were not there.

It is time we recognize how various events in our lives are happening for clear and specific reasons. My husband may have thought he was interested in seeing what was on the news, but actually, he was there as a result of a Higher Power at work who knew the need to have him present at that moment to allow for the manifestation of a miracle in the earth on that particular day. There is a synchronicity of events occurring twenty-four hours a day, seven days a week in our lives, but we usually don't notice them as such because we are too busy with our lives to pay attention to these perfectly timed events.

⁘

While lying unconscious in the hospital, I could hear the doctors discussing my status. I heard them speaking while standing on the right side of my bed about how to enter to repair the Aneurysm that had ruptured to save my life, but it appeared they didn't have a clue as to how to successfully fix the problem. I could feel and hear their sense of hopelessness.

Shortly after they left the room, another doctor approached my bed from the left side, yelling, "Mrs. Hunt, you have had an Aneurysm, and I can fix it!" Well, I knew what I heard from the other doctors that were in my room prior to him, so I asked him how confident was he that he could fix it. He replied, "Very Confident."

Now keep in mind, I was unconscious, so I really can't explain how this conversation took place, I just recalled it taking place as I have recorded it. I don't remember seeing the doctor; I just recall hearing him and replying to him. Apparently, I somehow gave him the okay because he took me immediately from wherever I was in the hospital to the operating room. I recalled opening my eyes for a split second once I was in the room where the surgery was going to be performed. I saw a lot of what appeared to be computers, and I remembered thinking, "Oh, what they do surgery with computers now?"

These are the events as I remember them, which is why I caution people if your loved ones are unconscious to be very careful what people are allowed to say around them as they can hear you even if they can't respond; and be intentional in speaking life to them in your attempts to assist them in regaining consciousness.

I had no clue how long surgery was, but I know it was successful. That doctor really did know his stuff, as I got many compliments about his work. I am not quite sure how many days I spent in the hospital, but I know it wasn't that many, as the moment I was awake and conscious, the hospital began immediately informing me I didn't have any health insurance. I recalled telling them, "I do," as I had just signed up with Obamacare during open enrollment in

November 2013.

I remember after finding myself in the hospital; thinking how grateful I was I had signed up, but the hospital couldn't find any record of my having insurance, so they were trying to kick me out. I just had major life-threatening emergency surgery to repair a ruptured Aneurysm, and the hospital was really trying to put me out for lack of insurance. They went back and forth with me about me not having insurance until they finally made the decision to send me home in my condition. I was very afraid; I didn't know what would happen to me, so once they released me, I had my family take me directly to Kaiser Permanente from the hospital, as that's who I chose when I signed up for Obamacare.

Fortunately, they were more sensitive. They explained there was a huge technical glitch with the Obamacare system; therefore, a lot of people who selected them were not showing up in the system, so as a courtesy, they agreed to see me until the confusion could be straightened out. This was when I discovered that the hospital had released me with a fever and lack of medication, so I concluded they sent me home to die, but my God had a different plan.

The attending doctor for Kaiser informed me I should have been given another prescription from the hospital which he provided. I went home to rehabilitate, and of course, I had to be taken back to the hospital several times, and each time I had to be transported by ambulance. I started experiencing what they term "Vertigo;" it's a condition where without warning, my bedroom would begin spinning around, causing me to feel like I was on a Carnival ride without a seatbelt. I had never in my life experienced anything like this before, and it scared me half to death. The hospital would examine me, prescribe medication, and send me back home.

<hr/>

While home recovering from all this emotional and physical trauma, I heard the voice of the Lord say, **"Get your medical records and read them."** I began asking how do I get my medical records, and low and behold no sooner I asked the question I discovered an unopened piece of mail on my bed. Upon opening it, I found instructions on how to get my medical records from this particular hospital. Wow, another synchronicity event at work on my behalf. Look at God, "Won't He Do It… YES HE WILL!"

I went online and followed the instructions and got my medical records. Upon reading them, one thing I discovered about the medical profession is they might not tell you everything, but they will document it in your file. I read how they discovered I had an enlarged heart, which I don't recall anyone ever telling me about. Yet, it was written in my medical records, and they indicated the matter was discussed among other doctors, but nothing indicating they ever discussed it with me.

While I am not a doctor, I couldn't understand the blood work, but it didn't take a rocket scientist to know something was wrong when the blood count read "200," and the normal range showed it should be between say, 7 – 16. I saw several blood readings like that, another read "300," and the normal range was from say, 3 – 12.

I saw enough to know they really did send me home to die. They sent me home after a lifesaving surgery to repair a ruptured Aneurysm with blood count readings such as these earlier than they should have for what appeared to be lack of insurance.

Listen, there are divine synchronicity of events happening every day in our lives if we would only pay attention to them. This is why no one can tell me my God is not real because no sooner I was reading over my medical records as He instructed; I received a call from my primary care doctor, who treated me when I was kicked out of the hospital, informing me he needed me to see an Endocrinologist as he was very concerned about the results of my blood work. So he informed me he had scheduled me to see one the next day and provided me with her information.

Well, after getting off the phone with him, I got on the computer to look up Endocrinologists as I didn't have a clue who they were or what they do. I wanted to have as much knowledge as possible to be able to have an intelligent conversation with her during my scheduled appointment.

While researching Endocrinology, I came across a book written by Dr. Michael L. Johnson entitled, *"You Can Beat Thyroid Disorders Naturally! The Ultimate Guide Using Natural*

Protocols," another synchronicity. I was led to download and print the pdf copy of this book, and I read it that day. At the back of the book, the doctor provided his personal contact information for those who wanted to contact him, so of course, I did. I took a chance on him responding to me and sent him a copy of my medical records via email and asked him for his professional opinion.

To my surprise, he responded the same day. He replied, "Mrs. Hunt, you have a lot of serious medical issues going on right now, I would recommend you start by detoxing your Liver." I was blown away because no one said anything to me about my Liver, but I took his advice. He is in partnership with a company that creates natural herbal remedies, so I went on his website and ordered the protocols he recommended in his book, and I started using them.

Yes, I had to work on healing myself as the local hospital had refused to assist me any further for what they thought was a lack of insurance. So, I started his protocols to detox my Liver, and I followed up with the Endocrinologist. I was able to get various herbs from his website to completely detox my system. I used his Liver-ND, Max B-ND, Body Mud Mask Detox, Medi-Dental Pack, B-12, D3 serum, you name it, I got it and used it.

As I began to get stronger to where I could get up out of bed without assistance, I was then divinely led through a series of synchronicity events to my next level of products to assist in my healing. I was on the internet, and an ad popped up on my screen advertising a free essential oils class at a location near me, I was led to attend. It was so informative, teaching how essential oils were very good for healing the body, so I began incorporating essential oils into my daily regimen of healing products, and before I knew it, I was feeling good as new.

❧∿❧∿❧

Through this process, I saw a whole lot of doctors and received a battery of tests, and one thing I want to note here is how every doctor that examined me spoke highly of the work the surgeon performed on me. I thought this peculiar; as I could see hearing maybe one or two compliments, but when I tell you EVERY doctor who examined me, and as I noted there were many, individually complimented the work of the surgeon. Stay with me here, as there is a reason I am highlighting this fact.

There came a point when my insurance changed, and I had to see another group of doctors and specialists who accepted my new insurance. It seemed like I was having to go through everything all over again, as I begin seeing an entirely different team of doctors who all took me through another extensive round of testing.

At one of my appointments with one of the new doctors, I had the same experience as with all the others. It started with his X-ray technician asking me who did my surgery as he was so impressed with the work. When he looked at my records and saw the name of the surgeon, he said, "Oh yeah, I'm familiar with his work!" He and the doctor must have really had serious discussion concerning it because as soon as the doctor entered my room, he too gave accolades about my surgery.

This particular doctor was so intrigued he asked a lot more questions about it. He then asked me if I would allow him to reopen my wound. I asked him why, and he said, "I want to make sure everything is sealed tight, that there are no leaks." I asked him couldn't he tell that from various scans and other tests, but he thought it would be better if he went back in.

While I really did not feel good about this at all, I had made a promise to my God that I would not fight whatever treatment I needed, as I come from a long line of women who did not believe in the medical profession and would not submit themselves to treatments of any kind. So, I agreed, and he scheduled the procedure a month out.

Now, I was very uneasy about this decision; I really did not want him to reopen my wound. I was so uneasy until my husband suggested I get in touch with the surgeon who originally did the work to get his opinion. I told my husband it was emergency surgery, so I didn't know who he was. Then remembering the X-ray technician who saw the name of the surgeon in my record caused me to turn to my records to get the name of the doctor who performed my surgery to call him. I had to leave a message for him to call me back as he was busy, so I did. He returned my call around 6:00pm that evening.

I told him who I was and explained to him what was going on, and he asked me why the doctor wanted to reopen my wound. I explained what the doctor told me, then he asked me what I was doing the next morning. I said, "Whatever you need me to do." He asked if I would come into his office in the morning early, he would examine me without charge and give me his professional opinion. He agreed without charge as he did not accept my new insurance.

Needless to say, I was in his office bright and early the next morning. I thought it very interesting he sent two doctors in to examine me before he came into my room, but it didn't matter to me, as he was doing me a favor and he wasn't charging me. When he entered my room, he introduced himself and said, "Mrs. Hunt, first I must tell you, I DID NOT do your surgery that is not my signature, but I will give you my professional opinion. If I were you, I would not allow him to reopen your wound." I thanked him and immediately called the other doctor and canceled the procedure and never went back to that doctor again.

Now it was very interesting this doctor said he didn't do my surgery, but he was listed as the one who did. It really didn't matter to me as I knew while people might think I'm crazy, I always felt it was an Angel who performed my surgery hence all the accolades, and this to me just confirmed it, so I left it alone.

I knew it was an Angel because there was something unique about the way he approached me from the left side of my bed, the way he and I were communicating, and because of what I saw when I opened my eyes for that brief moment in the operating room. All that technology, it looked like something beyond this world. I always felt deep within, the doctor who wanted to reopen my wound was interested in studying my surgeon's work up close and personal, which was his motive for wanting to reopen the wound. Remember, I only agreed to the procedure because of my promise to God that I would not fight against my doctors' recommended treatments. These events unfolded to show us how God will always give us Victory while exposing the tactics that could cause us defeat. "Won't He Do It… YES HE WILL!"

Finally, I was at a place wherein I wanted to get back to work to see if I were really okay and could handle working again, so I signed up with a temporary employment agency to get work at short term intervals. This worked pretty good for me as I felt I was easing my way back into the workforce.

After doing several short-term assignments, I accepted a yearlong assignment as an Administrative Sales Assistant with a major health insurance company. This was very exciting for me as it gave me an opportunity to see the inside workings of these big insurance companies after all I had experienced with my insurance dilemma. I thoroughly enjoyed it. I was hired to work for two female Managers who oversaw $300,000,000.00 in accounts. This was truly a blessing to me, as these two ladies worked circles around not only me, but many people I know.

These were two older women, one was 68 years old, and I believe the other was 71, and it was amazing to see them not miss a beat. These ladies worked harder than teenagers; their work ethic was impeccable. They had been working together for years and had become best friends. They shared many of their stories with me; this was indeed a divine assignment, as it provided the encouragement I needed to know that all was not lost for me at the age of "54."

These women were thorough in the handling of their accounts, they did personal site visits, which took them all over the state regularly, and they knew their accounts like the back of their hands. I really admired these two ladies as they provided me with much hope for my future, and what a blessing to be working for them after all I had just come through.

I was a little over the halfway mark of my work contract when my Managers wanted me to consider being hired permanently. I really loved working with them, but my personal life was falling apart. I was about to lose the house my family and I were living in, so I was making plans to move back to Georgia at the end of my contract to live with my younger children who were still there.

One afternoon, just a couple of months before the end of my work contract, I received a call from my primary care doctor while at work. She was frantic, I literally had to calm her down. She asked if I was able to go see a Specialist, as my blood work had come back abnormal. I told her I could do whatever she needed me to do. She said, she would set it up for me and call me back with the details, which she did.

I went to see the Specialist the next morning, and I asked him what was going on. He explained, "Whenever someone's blood numbers are as high as yours, it indicates there is cancer somewhere." He went on to explain, "Or it could simply be your system, and the numbers could automatically readjust to normal, but I would have to order further testing to know for sure."

During this time in my life, things were falling apart. I was on the verge of becoming homeless and transitioning to another state, along with the fact he wanted me to do the leg work to find out which companies accepted my insurance for the test he would need; all contributed to my not realizing the seriousness of my condition.

I honestly forgot all about what that Specialist had said to me, and I focused my attention on relocating to Georgia. Just before my assignment was up, my husband and I did become homeless; we spent one night under the bridge prior to spending the last two weeks before transitioning to Georgia, with his sister on her living room floor.

On my last day at work around 3:00 pm, the day my husband and I were scheduled to leave for Georgia that evening, I got a call from him. I could hear in his voice he was ecstatic about something, so I listened. He explained that he just got a job; he was going back to work with his previous employer.

Now, one of the concerns I had with this was I always felt he could go back to that employer at any time, but his pride wouldn't let him, so he elected instead to allow us to lose everything. Then he decides it's time to go back to work with them on the day we are scheduled to relocate to Georgia. This was my thinking; I promise I did not express it to him. I was excited for him, but I told him I was not willing to change my plans of going to Georgia.

He agreed and said he didn't expect me to and that he would still take me there, but he wanted me to know he was coming back to start his job. As planned, when I got off, we rested and got on the road around 11:00 pm headed for Georgia. Once in Georgia, he rested up and took the trip back to his job 700 miles away. I didn't understand why it happened this way, but I knew it was the divine plan of my God for it to be this way, so I just flowed with it.

<hr />

After being with our children a short time, I fell ill. I thought it was the flu, so I started doctoring myself up with over the counter medicines. The next day I got a pain in my abdomen, so I asked my son to call the ambulance as I couldn't take the pain. I was transported to the nearest hospital, wherein they began immediately running tests.

As I lay in the hospital bed awaiting my results, I never would have thought I would get the results they brought me.

After having four different teams of doctors visit with me, one doctor came in to inform me I had Leukemia, and he asked if I mind him sending me to a specialty hospital. I gave him permission, and he instructed me to relax, noting he would take care of everything to get me transported.

WOW, what a blow! As I lay in the bed awaiting transport, I heard the spirit of the Lord speak to me, saying, ***"This is not unto death but to bring you to a place of wholeness and wellbeing."*** I held to those words through my entire process, even though I had no clue why I was going through all of this; I simply accepted it as my journey to travel.

The pain in my abdomen was another synchronicity event used to get me to the hospital as my doctor later in my treatment asked, "How is the pain in your abdomen?" I explained to him I never felt it again, and he replied, "Good because it had nothing to do with your Leukemia."

I realized had it not been for the pain, I would not have gone to the hospital; I would have continued trying to treat myself with over the counter medicines. And I believe had I stayed in Maryland, I would not have survived Leukemia, as obviously that's what I had when I saw the Specialist there who did not diagnose me. "Won't He Do It... YES HE WILL!"

SELF-REFLECTION

My transformation journey began with the events outlined in this Chapter.

- What process(es) have unfolded in your life that you can identify as the beginning of your transformation journey? In what ways can you see God's hand at work in it?

- Have you had personal experiences with Angels? If so, describe them.

- How has this Chapter helped you identify events in your life as a preparation process for something greater?

*"And he said unto me, My grace **is** sufficient for thee: for my strength is made perfect in weakness. Most gladly therefore will I rather glory in my infirmities, that the power of Christ may rest upon me."*

(2 Corinthians 12:9)

Chapter 2

DEFEATING CANCER,
SURVIVING LEUKEMIA

U nlike my experience in the last chapter of being hospitalized, this time, I really didn't have any health insurance as I had just relocated to Georgia, but my treatment and stay was nothing like what I experienced in the last chapter. Ironically, to the contrary, I was treated like a queen.

I was given an amazing team of Oncology Specialists while at the same time given a Specialist for each major organ of my body, i.e., Cardiologist, Pulmonologist, Hepatologist, etc. as it was necessary to immediately and aggressively start me on Chemotherapy and Radiation treatments, and these drugs are known to have a negative effect on those organs so as a precaution, they were sure to have everyone in place for the purposes of monitoring my condition. Oh my God, to say those drugs are hard on the body is a vast understatement.

I spent months at a time in the hospital due to this disease. I was extremely sick, and the only thing worse than being this sick is finding yourself in this condition, and you look up, and no one's there with you. I was married, yet my husband was in another state living his life while I was fighting for mine, and he didn't have a clue. I had our four youngest children here who were working hard to keep a roof over their heads while taking care of their sick mother.

My youngest son was 19, sharing an apartment with his 21-year-old sister and her toddler, and my twenty-four-year-old was taking care of his family. My other son was 26 years old, sharing an apartment with a roommate, my son from another mother. This illness took its toll on all of them. My older children lived 700 miles away.

When I speak about having no one with me, I am not talking about my children, as they were awesome! I was so proud of them being so young when their mother fell ill to Leukemia and watching them step up to the plate to care for me. I marvel at their strength and maturity; this experience certainly allowed me to see them all in another light. I could not have been prouder; I will always cherish them for the unconditional love they displayed.

I am actually talking about the fact I was married, and I think at this point, I had been married for twenty-seven years, and we had been together for thirty-one, yet I did not have my husband by my side. I'm talking about being the seventh of eight children, and not having any of my siblings with me.

It's something about when you're down, especially due to illness, you long to be surrounded by those who are supposed to love you. I will not delve into this right now as much of it will be covered in the next chapter, but I will note here, LOVE, when it's pure and genuine, is a powerful healing balm, and it's FREE. I believe it can heal

ANYTHING!

I found myself in the fight of my life on a journey that would take me three years to get through. Now mind you, I almost lost my life last year after suffering a ruptured Aneurysm in which I had to fight to recover from, and now I found myself flat on my back again with another deadly illness seeking to take my life.

As I found myself bombarded with harsh pharmaceuticals around the clock, the only thing on my mind was, "What must I do to defeat this enemy (Inner-me)?" Unlike last year and unbeknown to me, this battle would be much harder to win as it was a disease that had invaded my bloodstream.

The medications used to fight this disease on a daily basis made me sick as all outdoors every time I took them, but they were the chosen method thought to be the best to fight the disease that had attacked my system. I know there are many opinions around whether or not Chemotherapy or Radiation should even be used as treatments. While I have experienced them both, I honestly don't know how I feel about the discussion.

I will take this opportunity to say I am not a medical professional, but I seek to offer my personal opinion here. I am of the mindset there is nothing like the God-given natural remedies we have for use in this earth, but I will also say, I believe the utilization of them has to be a lifestyle practice, not just something to turn to after a life-threatening diagnosis.

I personally believe the holistic natural way is best overall for our health in totality, but I also believe if you try to use its method only after being diagnosed with a life-threatening illness, it could prove dangerous as at that point you will have to know the intricate details of what is happening within your body and be able to provide the correct dosage while at the same time knowing exactly which herb is needed to fight whatever is happening in your body in order to have a chance at getting the successful results you seek.

At the point of being diagnosed with a life-threatening disease, I personally believe you should have already been working closely with a bonafide herbal holistic professional skilled in the area of chronic diseases if that is the route one is looking to take once diagnosed with a deadly illness. As with the pharmaceuticals, the Holistic Practitioner must have a working knowledge of the Anatomy and a thorough knowledge of herbs and how they interact with the Anatomy.

I have learned through this process how amazingly resilient this body is we live in; our bodies are perfectly designed to keep us alive while on earth. I believe chemotherapy and radiation serve to prove the power and uniqueness of our bodies. I witnessed my body being broken down into the weakest of weak vessels after the use of these drugs, and I watched it restore itself to full strength and vitality with the support of natural herbs and rituals.

My first months battling this disease was the hardest as the treatments were foreign to my system. I can remember my first round of chemo upon arrival at the specialty hospital. It was given intravenously, and I could feel it going into my vein through the IV, and my system burned within as it traveled through seeking to destroy the cancer cells that were out of order. There were nights I felt like my insides were burning up. I resented the times I was scheduled to get it because my insides felt like it was on fire every night after my treatment.

Looking back, I realize how truly amazing this body is to endure such agony and yet still keep the inner harmony amongst all the other organs inside now effected by the foreign chemicals entering its space to fight the erratic cancer cells that have become out of order.

⚜

While I was experiencing a lot of physical challenges with this disease, I was also enjoying several spiritual experiences at the same time. On several occasions, I recall having out-of-body encounters wherein I was flying around literally being guided to certain areas and enlightened concerning something specific about each location.

One night I was taken from my hospital room to a place I was familiar with that being my church. I landed in the balcony of my church when the Lord spoke to me and told me to dance; He said as I dance, the church will become full again. It was such a beautiful experience. Another day I was taken to a very high mountaintop. I was dressed in a very beautiful gown glistening with what appeared to be multi-color sparkles.

I was so free and feeling great when I sensed the Lord beckoning me to fall from the mountain into His arms. He said He wanted me to trust Him, so I did, and my dress opened so beautifully. The sparkles fell off in midair, creating an extraordinary scene of a sparkling array of colors as I gracefully floated in the air.

There was yet another time I was taken out, and this time I landed inside a building in a room where there was a meeting going on. This was like what they illustrated in the movie Scrooge, only as I stood watching and listening I commented about what was being said, and the facilitator heard me and responded to what I said. I then heard the Lord say, ***"They were not supposed to hear or see you,"*** and immediately I was yanked from that location back into my body in the hospital room. I can tell you I received very powerful information that I am not at liberty to release in this book, but will be sharing as I am sent to teach throughout the world.

I learned there are so many things we do in the name of the Lord that we believe is what God wants us to do only to discover from God it is not of Him. My mind was blown at the things we practice in the name of Jesus that God revealed to me is not of Him. We are living in the dispensation of time wherein everything, not of God, is being exposed. This process went on for about two months.

Finally, I was able to go home for the first time and do outpatient care at the Infusion Center. Oh my God, to think I had to show up at the Infusion Center every day was mind-blowing. Nevertheless, I was extremely happy to be home. It was sad for me that my nineteen-year-old son had to help me to the bathroom and assist me while in there because he and my daughter were all I had at that time, but I was tremendously grateful I had them. He never once complained, he would enter my room in the middle of the night to make sure I was okay and didn't need anything, and for that, I am truly grateful.

My twenty-one-year-old daughter elected to give up her bedroom to me while she and her baby girl slept on the couch during my recuperation. I was so proud of these two young people as they were awesome through the process, and neither of them ever made me feel I was a burden as parents so often think when they find themselves in conditions wherein they must depend on their children.

I remember watching them and listening while lying in bed as they discussed their schedules for taking care of me. I was so very proud of them! They demonstrated their unconditional love for their mother through this process. As I began to get stronger and able to get around with the assistance of an adult walker, I was happy; I felt like I was making some progress. I still had a very long way to go, but any amount of progress I experienced was more hope for me because I had been down for so long.

At this point, I moved in with my 26-year-old and my son from another mother because they lived very close to my Infusion Center, which made it much easier for me. I am so grateful to have children who loved me so much they were willing to do whatever was necessary for my recovery. My son slept on his floor and gave me his brand-new bed for a year and six months.

By this time, my health really began to improve; although I lost all my hair, and my left hip did suffer from the treatments I received, I was getting stronger. The doctors recommended I get a hip replacement, but this was when I said absolutely not. I told my doctors I was too young for a hip replacement and suggested we find another remedy. They spoke to me about Stem Cell Transplant, informing me they could take my stem cells from another part of my body and inject them into my hip. I thought that was better than getting a hip replacement, but I still put it off as I wanted to see what I could do naturally to restore life back to my hip. I put the care of my hip on the back burner as I was still in treatment for Leukemia.

❧⚬❧⚬❧

As I progressed in my care, I began to read a lot of books and taking a lot of online classes as my way of reaching for life to make sure my mind was strengthened and functioning well.

I was led to **"We Move, Our Bodies KNOW Women's Embodiment Community, by Stefana**

Serafina, Founder of Intuitive Body and Dance, " and took a dance class via Zoom! Yes, while using an adult walker to get around, I came across this group online, and I was led by God to sign up.

What was amazingly intriguing about this is I got halfway through the program when I realized I had not needed the walker or anything to assist me in getting around anymore. I was thoroughly ecstatic; it blew my mind because I did not even recognize it as it was happening.

This class was not an ordinary dance class; it was an inner workings class wherein we learned how to communicate with our bodies, how to listen to what the body was wanting to express. We took a deep dive into our Womb excavating all the deep old hurts we stored there; this was a very interesting experience. The instructor would lead us into a deep meditation with music and her soothing voice of instructions.

Once we arrived mentally down in our Womb, she would tell us to ask our Womb, *"What parts and shapes have I held tight and closed in my body for too long? What pain and what sorrow have I buried deep in my Womb that are ready to erupt with volcanic proportion? And from the heart of my Womb, what in me is ready to stand, take space and shape, and become a Giant to not be ignored?"*

WOW, we would go through a series of these meditations, and perform certain strategic body movements, it was awesome! I can't explain why or how it helped my hip because I certainly didn't consciously take the class for my hip, I was just led by God to take the class, so I did. All I know is I eventually no longer needed assistance to get around anymore after fully participating in this class and have not needed any assistance to this date, and I never had hip surgery or stem cell transplant. Thanks, but no thanks. I'm good! "Won't He Do It... YES HE WILL!"

⤧⤳⤲⤱⤰⤯

I was later led by God to take this awesome online course entitled, "**Chakra Energy Healing with Doreen Virtue.**" This course taught how our Chakra system could be used to realign whatever is out of order within our bodies. This class was very fascinating, oh my God, I learned how to move energy around within my body.

I discovered stagnant energy in the body can cause havoc to our anatomy as the body is designed to allow energy to flow freely throughout. What was unique about this course is it taught me how to charge my Chakras, it showed me how to use gems stones from God's amazingly awesome earth along with colors, essential oils, certain food groups, and meditation to strengthen each Chakra.

I learned what each Chakra meant in relation to my life, and not only that, this course taught about God's Angelic Host and how they work with each Chakra, mind-blowing! Yeah, this course truly assisted in my healing more than I can tell you! All in all, I could see God was teaching me to take the limits off and shift my belief system, so I could open myself to a greater dimension of healing.

⌘

As I hinted to earlier in this Chapter, Love is a powerful force in our Universe, so I was now led to take a course entitled, *"Self-Love Mastery by Rikka Zimmerman;"* this was an in-depth look at the power of love and its vibratory effects on every area of our lives. It was an exhaustive course, moving us step by step through a process of exploring this power as a free-flowing energy we could tap to empower ourselves.

This course consisted of twelve Modules of extensive work around the area of love. It was loaded with a whole lot of information centered around forgiveness, providing the opportunity to return to Love within Self as opposed to searching for it outside of yourself. I was able to come to a place of really understanding that God is Love, and accepting that flowing with the love of my creator helped me to better understand myself as a co-creator with Him in this finite Universe.

The awesome thing about this course is you were matched with an accountability partner to walk with you and help you practice the modules of the class, and my partner was from Poland! This was so exciting for me because I never met anyone from Poland; we met and got acquainted over Skype.

We did all our assignments via Skype; she was who I

called my Divine Covenant Connection. She and I adored one another; we felt like we were a perfect match. I would have never met her if it were not for this class. While some may be wondering how this relates to "Defeating Cancer; Surviving Leukemia," I would say it had everything to do with my recovery. The content of this class really strengthened me and supported my attitude through the process.

In fact, as I look back over all the classes I was led to take, they all played a vital part in my healing. Whenever you go through chemotherapy and or radiation treatments, you had better have a system in place to feed and elevate your mind because while your body is being ravaged, you need to be sure your mind is programmed to defeat the process. I actually began saying chemo and radiation are so powerful they reach deep down to your soul! Now that's some serious medications.

During this entire process, I am still in treatment, so I appreciated any help in keeping my mind off the treatment and how sick it made me every day. I continued taking courses; the next one I was led to was entitled, ***"Soulprint Healing for Affluence, Healing Your Family story of Lack, Pain, and Struggle by Carol Tuttle."*** Here was another course teaching about how to shift our energy fields for better living.

This one was full of exercises on how to maneuver our energy to receive the results we desired. It was all about connecting within, much of what I was learning I wished was taught when I was a child. This program taught me how to step out of my family's soulprint and into my divine soulprint, understanding that your parents' soulprint may be one of lack, pain, and struggle, or anything contrary to what you were created to flow in. I saw it as what we call in Christian dome, generational curses.

For the most part people do not realize they are continuing in the soulprint of their parents or lineage and they need to switch to their own God-given soulprint. This course taught how to make that switch. I knew nothing about any of these courses prior to being led to them by God, and it reminded me of when He said, ***"This is not unto death but to bring you to a place of wholeness and wellbeing."***

The more I journeyed through my process, I discovered it was doing just that. If you noticed, the courses I was led to all touched on my inner development. So, although my process didn't feel good at all, it was taking me somewhere while at the same time strengthening and equipping me for my divine purpose.

I want you to know we are all overcomers, but for the most part, our overcoming is usually overshadowed by those we believe or deemed are more important. I want to take this opportunity to give thanks and honor to all the overcomers, and I pray this living testament inspires you to tell your story because your story is just as important as the next, so I say rise up you mighty overcomer and let the world see your light through your story.

SELF-REFLECTION

I realize I have had what most might consider unorthodox experiences; nonetheless, they are mine. Now, I ask you to share yours:

- What thoughts and feelings arose that reminded you of how you defeated or survived circumstances you thought would take you out?

- What events can you now identify where supernatural provision was provided?

What, if any, out-of-body experiences can you recall having?

"And I will give this people favour in the sight of the Egyptians: and it shall come to pass, that, when ye go, ye shall not go empty."

(Exodus 3:21)

Chapter 3

BECOMING A DIVORCEE AFTER 33 YEARS

This Chapter was the hardest of all the Chapters to write, as it deals with love relationships which tends to be so misunderstood. I am committed to sharing in such a way in this Chapter to allow you to experience the creative energy surrounding the power of genuine love in relationships.

While my surviving a divorce after being together so long may encompass some details that may not be so pleasant, I will make every effort to capture the creative energy flowing naturally through relationships as I share my story. But first, I'd like to offer a disclaimer here: **"There is more than one side to every intimate relationship story. Each story consists of the perspectives of those involved, as well as the Truth of what's really going on or has gone on."** Remember, your perspective of things shows up as YOUR truth; herein lies my truth.

In order to get to my marrying and surviving 33 years in that relationship before ending it, I must share with you my humble beginnings. I should also reveal to you this was not my first marriage, and even before that, I should tell you a little about how I was raised.

I came through three generations of single moms who did the best they could with what they had; however, I believe there is a reason it takes two people, male and female, to create a child. It takes two to create the child because obviously, the child needs something from both persons to develop into his or her own unique personality. So likewise, it just makes sense that child will require something from each parent in growing up to become all he or she is designed to be in this world.

There are 22.4 million children being raised in single-parent households, according to the U.S. Census Bureau. I am of the belief that as a single parent, you are lacking something your counterpart is designed to contribute to the raising of the children, and therefore believe both parents should be equally involved in raising them. This is one of those situations in life I feel we take for granted as we continuously violate the law of creation by overlooking the need for both parents to harmoniously co-parent the children, we don't realize the consequences of this violation upon the lives of the children. Yet we wonder why some people seem to be so unstable in this life.

Every child's experience is different around the effects of an absentee parent, so I want to take this opportunity to share a little about mine. You see, I would not meet my father until I was eleven years old. As a child, I convinced myself he had a right to choose whether or not to be in my life, and he chose not to be, so I had to accept his choice in the matter and move on. As a little girl, I convinced myself of this as justification for him not being in my life. It made me feel better about him not being there by accepting that he exercised his God-given right (free-will) of choice not to be there.

Upon finally meeting him, he gave me $25 and took me out to the department store wherein I watched him purchase over $200 worth of clothing for himself, what an impression, and back in that time $200 got a lot of clothing. I remember seeing him put a lot of clothes on that counter.

What I did not realize was his absence planted a seed of abandonment and neglect within me that germinated and grew causing me to allow every man who entered my life to choose how they wanted to show up in my life, and I was already programmed by adulthood to believe I was to accept their choice and behaviors, and as a result, I literally tolerated almost anything.

For instance, allowing my first husband to marry me purchasing a 25 cents bubble gum ring to serve as my wedding ring, and that's another whole story in and of itself. This tolerance played out in all my relationships, and I had no clue what was going on until fairly recent while in a session with my Life Coach/Therapist, Melissa Edwards Brown, in which she was teaching on "Soul Wounds" that I learned as she taught that I suffered from the soul wound of abandonment. Oh my God, it was then my life flashed before me, and I could see clearly what had been happening in my life over the years.

She went on to show me how I had intellectualized my

emotions as a child for coping with my father's absence. WOW, this revelation was the beginning of a whole new level of freedom for me! It spoke volumes to the importance of both parents remaining in the lives of the children, as to have either not be present, open portals of invisible wounds that play out adversely in one form or another in the lives of the children.

⟜⟝⟜⟝⟜⟝

Continuing on with the sharing of my humble beginnings, I should tell you I am a fourth-generation woman conceived and raised in poverty. My great-grandmother lived on a slave plantation before moving into a community with her own ethnicity where men and women were married, running successful businesses and taking care of their families, but she didn't have anything and had to live with other families before becoming one of the first to move into what would be called Public Housing.

Unbeknownst to the community, this was the beginning of another cycle of poverty that would run through generations. It would become one of the hardest cycles to break away from, not just physically but mainly mentally only because it became a self-sustaining environment with separate rules for life that did not match the rules of the society at large or the laws of nature. It was the beginning of indoctrinating the minds and destroying any hopes of having a male and female household built on the principle of truth in the public housing environment because immediately following Public Housing came Public

Assistance, also known as Welfare.

One of the requirements for qualifying for Public Assistance was the male could not live with his family. So, while they did initially live together as a family, once the financial condition became such that the household needed further assistance and the woman applied to receive Public Assistance, it set in motion spiritual ramifications that would negatively affect generations to come. To receive financial assistance, the woman would have to lie about the man being absent, thereby creating a lifestyle of lying and cheating, and no one saw the correlation to how they would eventually live their lives with one another.

This is my perspective as a fourth-generation participant of both programs as my mother moved into Public Housing and participated in the receipt of Public Assistance (Welfare). She went on to raise eight of her children there, and when I became pregnant as a teenager, my mother put me on Welfare even thou the father was a responsible young man working and providing me with money every week.

When my great-grandmother died, I would be given her Public Housing unit, and the cycle continued until my awesome, amazing, magnificent God intervened on my behalf, but not before I would begin raising my children in it. "Won't He Do It... YES HE WILL!" I will explain how He did that later; but first I must now take you into how I met this man whom I would later marry and live 33 years with before divorcing.

To share with you how I survived, I have to tell you about how we met. I was what you called a homebody when I met my husband, meaning I was the sibling who did not party, drink, smoke, do drugs or gamble and was always home. I literally stayed in the house for most of my life unless I was going to school, work, or shopping. I was what I like to call the plain Jane of my family, you see, my siblings loved to party and could dance and sing circles around anyone.

Years would pass when I would meet someone, and once I told them who my siblings were, they would not believe me. They would always ask where was I when they were growing up, no one knew me. I want you to get the picture of how secluded my life was, and I personally believe it was by divine design. I believe my God preserved my life for such a time as this in His Kingdom. I believe, without a doubt, I am going to do great exploits because of my relationship with my God. While I spent most of my life alone, I was never alone or lonely! I would like to think I was my Father (GOD's) best-kept secret.

Well, we had a family friend who lived approximately 35 miles North of us who wanted to come and spend some time with our family for the weekend. Now mind you, I told you who I was in my family so please tell me why this young man insisted on staying with me for the weekend. He could have stayed with anyone in my family, i.e., my mother, who lived across the street from me, my sister, my brothers, you name it, but he insisted on staying with me. This is a powerful demonstration of the synchronicity of events leading up to me meeting and marrying my husband.

During this time, I was a mother of four very special children, separated from my first husband, and very content with my Life. I had decided I would focus on raising my children and manifesting the life I knew I deserved. I was not mad at anyone; it did not work between me and my first husband and I was moving on with my life as a single mother.

I was a reader, I read a lot of self-help books and listened to self-help tapes from Nightingale Conant. I was determined I would create a better life for myself. Please note, I had not yet invited Jesus into my life, which is why I did not mention reading of the bible, although I did read it occasionally.

Anyway, I decided to allow our family friend to stay with me. Now it was the day before he was to leave that I began to feel convicted because I had not done anything with him since his arrival. I learned there was going to be a surprise birthday party for one of my best friends across the street from me, so I made up my mind that I would take him over there, so he could have some fun before he returned home.

Upon arriving at my girlfriend's house, we entered her living room, which was filled with people on the dance floor. We walked through to her kitchen, wherein she and several other people were sitting around a long table, so I asked her if I could get some water. I noticed this guy practically breaking his neck to get me a glass of water, which I accepted. Later, this same guy asked if I would dance with him, so I did.

For me, it did not mean anything, as I was not interested in a relationship at this time. Little did I know this would be my next husband and the person I would spend the next 33 years of my life with. Unbeknownst to me, he begged my best friend for weeks to tell him where I lived because he was interested in talking to me, she eventually gave in and provided him my contact information.

The rest is history; he actually paid for my first divorce and went on to make me his wife. If our family friend did not insist on staying with me, I would never have been at that party wherein he and I met. I later discovered my husband and his cousin threw a party for my best friend every year, yet I never knew it, nor did I know them. Apparently, they were pretty close to my best friend, and our paths never crossed until this particular night. Again, I just want you to see the synchronicity of events at work and give you an idea of all the pieces of this puzzle that had to be brought together for my husband and I to meet!

⚜

He and I met and married in our twenties, and like most relationships wherein neither party know themselves or each other, test and trials showed up to reveal you. I was committed to making this marriage work, I was not aware that my husband wasn't as invested in our relationship. I would not accept this truth, yes, I said, "Accept" until many years later.

There were many signs from the start that I chose to ignore in the beginning, so it wasn't until after being married to him for more than 25 years that I would come face-to-face with this truth demanding I acknowledge it and respond, that I began to do just that. WOW, some may wonder, why did it take so long to accept what was not working in the marriage from the beginning?

I really want to take my time sharing right here so others going through or finding themselves in a place they don't yet know how to maneuver can glean from this Chapter, find their footing, and be set free be it inside or outside of the relationship.

Truth be told, there were signs early in my relationship, such as he did not have his own place. BAM, first red flag! As a man wanting to be in a relationship with someone, this showed a lack of responsibility which flowed throughout our relationship and also showed up in his judgment of life through the bad decisions he made during our time together. Responsibility is a huge skill needed in life, but especially when entering a relationship.

Second red flag, right out of the gate, he demonstrated his disrespect for order, thereby disrespecting me as I am a woman of order. I had my children fed, bathed and in bed by 8:00pm every night and I was right behind them and asleep by 9:00pm, and still, he called and came after 9:00.

I allowed my order to be disrupted by accepting this behavior, which directly correlates with what I learned as a child being abandoned by my father. This is not to blame my father, but to show patterns of behaviors we adapt from traumatic events in our lives. Order is a vital function of life; without it, things become disarrayed, be it physical or emotional.

It is these little things we should pay most attention to in relationship building because how you start a relationship is nine times out of 10, the determining factor whether the relationship thrives or dies. Which is why so many people find themselves in unhappy relationships blaming each other without recognizing the root cause of their problems.

Let it be known here, I was the one in violation. I gave up the principles I lived by to be in relationship with this man, whether consciously or unconsciously. Which is what usually happens in relationships, particularly with the woman being the one to give in to be in a relationship. By giving in, I mean, she sees there are things that really will not work for her, and she decides for the sake of being with this person she will accept it and hope things change or even believe she can make it change.

I know it is not always the woman who gives in, but we must be honest with ourselves, the majority of the time it is women giving in. This is why I admire men so much and recognize we can learn a lot from them when it comes to handling emotions, particularly in relationships, because men are wired differently and handle their emotions very different.

You can say women wear their emotions on their sleeves when it comes to relationships because we operate from our emotional side, which is not necessarily a bad thing as our emotions are a gift. However, we tend to allow our emotions to rule, overtaking us in relationships, wherein men are usually more in control of theirs.

Men don't allow their emotions to rule them in the way women do. Women tend to relinquish their power of choice to their emotions, thereby finding themselves more broken and nearly paralyzed when relationships go bad, while men move on, more in control of their lives, needing much less recovery time than women in a break-up.

I believe relationships fall apart because, unfortunately, most times we start out with blinders on, only seeing what we want to see and making excuses for what we call the smalls things. Therefore, the relationship ends up dissolving whether it's after seven years or 50 years, whether you are married or shacking up; it falls apart once either party awakens to the truth of what was always there, but ignored and now becomes an issue.

Some of the blinders we tend to put on are things like, i.e., "It won't happen to me," "He/She didn't mean to hurt me," "It won't happen again;" "I've been married before, so I am going to make this one work," "No one in my family is married so I have to make this work," "But I love him/her," "I can fix him/her," "He/she will change," "I've invested too much in it to leave," "We've been together too long to quit," or "It's going to get better," which was my favorite one, etc., etc., etc. Not to mention our religious beliefs coming forth from our subconscious mind, i.e., "God hates divorce," "What God has put together let no man put asunder," "My Vows say for better or worse," and the list goes on and on.

Now concerning the biblical points, please note I am not making mockery because they are true. However, God has given me much insight into them that differs from the interpretations we have been taught. Again, this is one of those items I will discuss openly as I do workshops around this book. Please know there are greater revelations around these truths, which unlocks us from the bondage of the religious interpretations that usually hold us hostage in our relationships.

My husband and I served as Elders in the church, and I can tell you some things my husband did to me that would make your head do a 360-degree spin, yes as an Elder of the church, which is another topic for another book. I promise you I did not realize my husband was living a double life in that he tried to live one way while at home, "The Christian life," but was partaking in all manner of stuff outside the home.

I will not share any details here but will share freely as I am invited to discuss this book around the world. I am free to discuss it all, and I believe it is necessary to have these sacred discussions wherein we open up and tell all to release the shackles of bondage from our lives and go FREE to do the perfect will of God. Secrets keep you shackled, clips your wings, and prevent you from soaring as you were designed to.

❧❧❧

Early in our marriage, he went on to have a child with another woman, but of course, he kept denying the child was his while at the same time never submitting to a blood test to prove it. Although we all know in order for there to be a possibility of fatherhood, you would have to be intimate with the person. Yeah, I forgave this man for so much stuff it would blow your mind, some stuff perhaps you and many others would say is unforgivable, but I believe in extending the olive branch to anyone in need of it.

The thing about the conception of this baby is the woman lived on the other side of our community, and I later learned that he was with this young lady when he tracked me down wanting to be in my life. He never stopped seeing this woman while he was married to me, and while he denies this, the proof is the child was conceived and born while we were married.

Once children are conceived, I believe it is God who ordains it to be so. All we have to do is think about couples who try for years to conceive children and do not, and then those who were told they would never be able to conceive and then they do. I just believe God is the determinant factor for whatever reason.

I have learned; we may not understand, like, or believe it, but the divine purpose of our lives can sometimes take us down paths we never thought we would go. Hosea, a prophet of God, was told by God to marry Gomer a whore, according to Hosea 1:2. God hardened Pharaoh's heart after giving Moses instructions for Pharaoh to follow, according to Exodus 7:13, and again the list can go on and on.

The point is, just because something may seem horrible or outside what we believe, does not mean it is not divinely ordained by God. According to scripture, it was God who invited Satan to attack Job, need I say more?

I will say, infidelity is a character flaw in my honest opinion, as it is not hard to be committed to someone you love. I am living proof as my entire time with my husband, and all that he took me through, I remained 100% faithful to him and the marriage, as did Hosea according to scriptures.

Now I will add, infidelity can be related to what was modeled before them, and my husband was a part of a community where infidelity ran rampant and appeared to be the norm. It is my understanding he watched men have multiple families on the same street, among other unacceptable behaviors he witnessed.

Even with that, I do believe my husband, as well as other people who struggle with being committed to one mate, must understand the power of choice is theirs to use, and they do, just not wisely, for the most part.

I believe it was the will of God for me to meet my husband because of the synchronicity of events leading up to our meeting. I also believe it was for the purpose of bringing forth his seed, which was the divine purpose we were brought together as I did birth five amazing children with him. The youngest two already have offspring and had things gone the other way with us earlier than it did, those two children would not be here, and therefore their seed would not have entered this earth realm.

Please, just think about that for a moment, the grandchildren that are already here from our youngest two children would not be here if things had gone the way it could have between my husband and I before their parents were conceived. God knows the purpose for which they are here and what their seed will bring to the earth or their seed's seed, but the truth is they had to get here in order to have an opportunity to release their seed into the earth.

When it comes to love relationships, we don't consider the unborn seed awaiting its opportunity to enter the earth. We merely operate from our feelings and make our decisions based on our finite emotions at any given time, never considering the seeds that have not been released. We forget we were put here to be fruitful and multiply, failing to realize sex is for the purpose of reproduction. I did not say intimacy, I said, "Sex is for the purpose of reproduction."

Our society has made it about everything except reproduction, which is why we have many of the problems we see in our world, particularly around rape and sexually transmitted diseases because, in our ignorance, we violate the purpose of sex, and therefore abuse it. There is so much truth in what Dr. Myles Munroe said, "If you don't know the purpose of a thing, abuse is inevitable." This truth can be applied to every area of our lives!

❦

Now, back to the time God took us out of public housing. One day, I was about to leave out of my public housing unit when my God stopped me in my tracks and began showing me on my wall, a motion picture starring my lineage.

The Lord pointed out to me how I had come through three generations of poverty, and that I represented the 4th generation of women in poverty. I fell on my knees right on the spot and began crying out, asking God to forgive my ancestors, myself, and anyone else involved for our ignorance of aligning with poverty. I asked God to let the buck stop here and let not another generation experience poverty in any form again.

After that intervention and prayer, it was less than 30-days, and the Lord moved us out of Public Housing into one of the wealthiest communities in our county. Talk about a miracle because my husband and I, together or apart, could not buy a glass of water with our credit.

I must share this testimony with you. It began when my husband was on his way back from a little league baseball practice with the boys when he spotted a house for rent.

Upon arriving home, he told me about it, he really wanted me to take a look at this house.

Well, I was very reluctant as one, I had never lived in a single-family house, and two, our credit couldn't buy us a glass of water. My husband was very sporadic when it came to the financial support of the family, but was good at creating debt, so our finances were a mess, get the picture? I made every excuse in the world not to see this house.

On another occasion, I was with him coming from little league practice, when we passed the house there was a line all the way out the front door down its walkway of people waiting to see this house. I really felt we didn't stand a chance with that many people interested, I complained about the line being too long to stop so we went home.

As destiny would have it, my husband would not let it go, so the following Sunday after church, he insisted we go see if the house were still available. I was nervous as all outdoors as I truly did not feel we would qualify to rent this house, but I followed my husband's promptings. We got out of the car, and as fate would have it, we met the owners at the garage of the house.

We asked them if their house was still available; the owners proceeded to look at my husband and I and tell us the house was ours. I laughed, they replied, "Honestly, the Lord said, you are the ones to have this house." I laughed like Sarah in the bible; only my laughter was audible. They said they were serious and proceeded to show us the house.

It was a beautiful four-bedroom house with a full basement. It had a kitchen, dining room, living room, laundry room, garage, and a special glass-enclosed family room with a fireplace and a Grand Piano, which they said they were leaving for our use. There was an exceptionally large fishpond filled with huge, beautifully colored fish in the back yard, which by the way, was extremely large, and all appliances were included.

They told us we were the ones to have their house without doing an application or credit check on us. At the end of our tour, they told us what they were asking for rent, monthly, and that there was no need to do a credit check, nor were they requiring a security deposit as the Lord said, **"You are the ones to rent the house."**

Well, take notes readers here is where the religious mind led by fear comes in. Immediately upon seeing how God was moving in this deal, "I," decided, "WOW, if God is working on our behalf like this, let me see if we can get the house I want." It had always been my dream of living in a split foyer, and there was one for rent in the community I always hoped to live in when I was a young girl.

So I, with my religious, fearful self, literally turned down this opportunity of a lifetime and told the owners we couldn't accept as we were working on another deal. Ha, I lied, I just knew the split foyer was available, but we had not put an application on it.

Please keep in mind, I didn't want to see this house

because I knew we weren't creditworthy, but here I am willing now to complete a credit application for another house because of what I just witnessed God doing for me with this house, so I thought it meant He would move on my behalf on the house I wanted.

Stupid, stupid, stupid, and more stupid! I really did this after witnessing the traffic of people viewing this house for an opportunity to rent it without having another sealed deal in my hand. I proceeded to get the information on the split foyer in the other community. Now the community where the house was, I had just turned down, was one of the wealthiest communities in our county. It had the best school district and I turned it down.

Let me take this time to expound upon what was happening here and the true motives behind my decision.

- Motive #1 - Fear, the number one culprit. In this case, it was an all-white community, and I simply was not ready to jump from public housing into an all-white community that was too much of a culture shock for me.

- Motive #2 - Wanting my Will to be done, not God's. I really did feel since God was moving so powerfully, He should give me what I wanted, so I opted to see if He would work that way.

- <u>Motive #3</u> - Self-Sabotage from an old belief system. Subconsciously feeling like I am not worthy of such elevation so quickly, I went into self-sabotage mode.

I mean, I completely turned it down without hesitation and with no other deal on the table. Who does that? Someone operating out of fear, wanting to have their own way, and operating in self-sabotage mode.

Well, I proceeded over to the community where the split foyer was located. I happily completed a credit application, provided a check for the security deposit and the fee for the credit checks, and waited for the results. It was approaching the end of summer vacation and the children being back in school through this process. I had less than three weeks for the children to return to school. Two weeks after putting in this application on the Split Foyer, I had not heard anything from the owner. I would call periodically and get no answer. One Saturday, I decided I would call back to back until he accepted my call, indicating I felt something was wrong. When the owner did pick up, I told him who I was and why I was calling. He replied, "I know who you are, and I'm not renting my house to you because you don't pay your bills," and he hung up the phone.

I began crying my eyes out on my bed as I was all packed to move, believing God was going to move us out of public housing. I felt like the stranded man on his rooftop during the flood wherein God had sent him a rowboat, motorboat, and a helicopter in response to his prayers, but he declined them all, not recognizing God answering his prayer. It was just a week before school started, and I did not have a place to move.

After a period of time with me crying, I heard the voice of the Lord ask, **"Are you finished crying? Now get up and call the people who own the first house back."** I got up, dried my eyes, and proceeded to look for their number. Realizing I had their number in my office at work, I got dressed and drove to my office, unlocked those doors, got their number, and called them.

I had to leave a voice message. I informed them of who I was and told them the deal we were working on fell through, and we wanted to know if their house was still available. The wife returned my call immediately, saying, "We told you this was your house," and she went on to explain, "After you all left, we told everyone the house was no longer available, that we had rented it." WOW! "Won't He Do It... YES HE WILL!"

Let me share with you what happened once we moved in. The first week after moving in, we heard a knock at our door, and upon opening it, we were greeted by a welcoming committee with freshly baked goods for us. It blew our minds as we had only seen this on TV.

Then we received a personal phone call from the school inviting us to a school fundraiser. You would never guess the price per plate. This community did not rely on government funds to do what they wanted done for their school. They pulled together as a community to raise the necessary funds they needed for school projects.

Well, this fundraiser was a $1500 per plate event! From Public Housing to the Palace, wouldn't you say! We gracefully bowed out of this fundraiser, noting we had just moved in, so we would like to pass on this one, and would look to participate in future fundraisers.

God is so faithful! We hosted our first Thanksgiving Dinner in our new home, wherein we invited our family and friends. We started counting the people as they came through; once we got to 75 people, we stop counting. To say the house was full is an understatement; we had people on every level of the house.

And remember that grand piano, well none of us could play it, but one of my uncles played piano all his life in church, and when he showed up, he lit up the house with Holiday music for the children as well as for the adults. It was an unforgettable celebration.

Shortly after this celebration, my uncle was found dead in his apartment of what appeared natural causes, talk about being grateful for having that time with him before he transitioned. I will always remember that gathering of love and celebration of life. It was truly amazing!

❧❧❧❧❧

Well, what do you do after moving into such an awesome house as this? One would think you settle in and get your finances straight, so you could purchase your own house, right? Wrong! The very next year, just before our lease was up for renewal, I overheard the children talking about how we should move to Georgia. Then, a couple of days later, my husband came home talking about God said we must move to Georgia.

I was upset, my first response was, "Well, He didn't tell me that!" I did not understand all this discussion about moving; we just moved out of public housing, why was there any discussion about moving? I was extremely happy here, and the owners had moved out-of-state, trusting us with their property. I said, "I'm not moving anywhere." When I tell you, I was kicking and screaming against the idea of moving. Plus, this move was not around the corner; it was 700 miles away!

I had fallen in love with this house, the community, and the school district, so there was no need to move except, I was told, "God said we must move to Georgia." I complained so much against it that my husband planned a trip to take me there to one of T.D. Jakes' "Woman Thou Art Loose Conferences." Here again, I must share with you the testimony of events that followed:

Several of us went on this trip to visit Georgia, my husband, the children, two of my brothers, and their wives. They made it a big event, while the women attended the Woman Thou Art Loose Conference, the men and children explored Georgia.

At the end of the Conference, we were traveling along

the interstate in a huge van when unbeknownst to anyone in the van, this big dark cloud entered through the front window, like something you see on TV, and went directly into my chest.

When I tell you, I became so scared that I did not say anything to anyone about what happened. I just told everyone we were ending this vacation, and going back to our hotel room to pack our things and hit the road. I was so afraid I completely cut the rest of the trip short without any explanation. I had become so full of fear, I told everyone that was it for Georgia, and I did not want to hear any more discussion about us moving there!

Now, we later discovered on the news, as we were packing, someone committed suicide by jumping off the overpass onto the highway we were traveling just before we came through. I wondered if that was what the dark cloud was, I do not know, all I know is I never experienced anything like it before in my life.

Well, about two weeks had passed, and I was on the phone talking with Pastor Boyer, a good friend of mine, the conversation was so enlightened that I felt comfortable explaining to him what happened to me when I was in Georgia, how this dark cloud came out of midair through the front window directly into my chest, and how I was immediately filled with fear.

He listened very intently, and once I finished, he kindly said, "Now Joyce, you must ask yourself, what's in Georgia the devil doesn't want you to have?" As soon as the last word fell from his lips, I literally felt the shackles of fear break off me and fall to the floor, and I was free to go into my prayer closet and ask God about Georgia and all this conversation surrounding it, and I did just that.

I went into my prayer closet with a list, and I said, "God is this you wanting me to go to Georgia? You just moved us out of public housing into this beautiful house, and I just got a letter from my employer announcing I will be getting a pay raise in two weeks, etc., etc., etc."

And as my God always does, he answered. He said, **"Yes, it is I, and you can stay here in Maryland, and I will sustain you, or you can follow me and get what I have for you."** At that point, with no further discussion I wrote out my two weeks' notice of resignation and took it in to the office the very next day as I am always of the mindset, I want what my God has for me.

Upon submitting my resignation, the following morning, my boss was stunned and reluctant to accept it. He was extremely concerned for me as he recalled I had been through a lot with my husband. How, one day I had come into work only to have a nervous breakdown in his office, wherein I couldn't stop crying uncontrollably, nor could I tell him what health insurance I had so he could get me some help. How he literally had to call HR to get my information and personally take me to see a therapist because of what I was going through with my husband. He also knew my faith in God, when I told him I heard from God and that I had to go, he accepted my resignation.

⥄⥄⥄

I went to Georgia because it was my desire to get all that God had for me, and since He said it was Him, I followed. It was truly an amazing experience as My God met me every step of the way. From my third day after arriving in Georgia, being at the clinic getting the children the mandatory Ear, Eye, and Throat exams for school.

A Nurse walked into the room to tend to the children, and she looked at my husband and I and said, "You two need a house, don't you?" My husband and I both looked at each other. She went on to describe a house to us and asked if we wanted to see it. She said she knew so much about the house because she owned it. She gave us the address and scheduled for us to see it later that evening.

My husband and I set the GPS and journeyed out to see it. As we traveled through a subdivision, our eyes bucked, and we both said, "Is God placing us in this community?" The GPS led us through to the back of this subdivision, which was an entrance to another subdivision. As we entered that subdivision, it was much more beautiful than the one we passed through, so we really got excited, and yes, low and behold, this was the subdivision where the house was located. We parked the car and rang the doorbell; the Nurse answered the door and welcomed us in.

Listen, this house was jaw-dropping beautiful! She walked us into the kitchen where her husband was preparing

60

dinner and introduced us. When her husband turned from the stove to look at us, he stumbled and almost fell. He would later share with us what that was all about, I will explain in a moment.

The Nurse gave a complete tour of this immaculate, beautifully designed four-bedroom home. The kitchen opened to the sunken family room with a fireplace, it had separate breakfast and dining areas, a laundry room, and a two-car garage. It had a very nice large flat backyard, which was great because Georgia appeared to be hilly. This was a new subdivision and an awesome dream house.

They explained to us they were having another house built in this same subdivision that would not be available for another six weeks, so we would have to wait until then to take possession. They also explained their plans to give this house to their daughter, who would not be ready for another year, so the rental would only be for one year.

We explained to them neither of us was working yet. They were people of faith, so they said with confidence, "Not a problem, you will be working soon." They drew up the agreement, and we executed it. We would live in this awesome house for our first year in Georgia. The husband explained to us when he turned and saw me standing in his house, he stumbled and almost fell because God had just shown him me in a vision the night before. "Won't He Do It... YES HE WILL!"

For the most part, whenever God speaks to us or have one of His servants speak to us, in our minds, we tend to believe it to be our definition of good. However, I can testify that the journey God has for us does not always look or feel like what we understand as good. Nevertheless, it is indeed good for us.

Everything we experienced since arriving in Georgia had been incredibly good and exciting. My husband went on to establish his own business, and I was in real estate; life was good for us. However, you never know what's lurking in the dark. Remember my husband's lifestyle that I was not aware of when we met, well what is done in the dark, and never confessed, will be brought to light.

My husband hired an assistant to work with him in the business, and things seemed to be good. What I did not see was my husband went on to have an affair with his assistant, allowing her to drive my car, going to her house on their lunch breaks, etc., etc., etc. I didn't have a clue, I did not know what was going on until one day I had some papers to fax on a real estate deal, and his shop was closer for me to stop by and use his fax machine than for me to run to my real estate office, so I did.

I had the children in the car with me as I had just picked them up. As we pulled up to the front entrance of his shop, I noticed one of his buddies standing in front of his door and a parked car, which I pulled up beside had two females in it, but I just noticed them, I really didn't think anything about it. I entered his shop, greeted him, and told him I needed to fax some papers.

He was changing out of his work clothing. I still didn't think anything strange was going on, so I finished what I had come there to do, kissed him, and told him I was on my way home and I would see him later.

As I exited his shop, and upon entering my car, OUR CHILDREN were having an all-out conversation about the assistant who worked with their father. I did not realize she was in that car I parked beside. My children were not saying anything nice about her, and I asked them why they were saying they did not like her.

My daughter said, "Because of the way she dresses, she always has her breast hanging out; she looks like someone who would have sex with daddy knowing he's married." Then the others chimed in on the conversation, and I was floored. My children spent a lot of time at his shop, and apparently, he exposed them to quite a bit. They told me how he let her drive my car and our son's car.

I was devastated hearing the things my children were telling me. I could not believe that my husband was so thoughtless to expose our children to his choice of bad behavior, but then again, I had actually been through worse with him, so I really should not have been surprised, but I was. I was really shocked at the conversation our children were having about this woman and their father.

Well, my showing up unannounced to his shop that evening exposed a whole lot as he was changing his clothing because he and his friend were about to go out on a double date which they did. However, my husband ended up cutting the date short after I showed up unannounced to the shop.

Of course, I proceeded to ask my husband questions about the things revealed to me by our children. I told my husband he had to fire the "B." Yes, I referred to her as a female dog, but to add insult to injury, that husband of mine had the nerve to come to her defense by telling me not to call her that. WHAT! I was heart-broken, if you never experience such a thing, you cannot imagine the pain I felt. I have always been faithful to my husband, but he had never been faithful to me. With all I had been through with him over the years, I would have never thought it would come to this; yet, actually, this was the beginning of our end.

❧≈∾∞∾≈☙

When you think about how God told me to go to Georgia to get what He had for me, look at what I got in my obedience. Yes, there were great and mighty things I experienced, but at the end of the day, my marriage was dismantled, and I actually had to move back to Maryland to regroup.

I have learned that what is good for us may not always look or feel good to us, but if it is from our God, you can guarantee it will always work out for our good. While I am not saying God ordered this behavior my husband was displaying, I do believe He set the appointed time of exposing it.

I believe my God had given my husband enough time to change his ways, and I believe God said enough is enough. I always tell people God's grace does run out, and you do not want to ever get to a place where you allow God's grace to run out on you before you obey Him.

I came to realize a whole lot of other households were experiencing what I had experienced as I heard horror stories from people in relationships, including those who were married and in the household of faith. I began to ask God about infidelity, and the crisis in relationships surrounding it.

He began to give me insight into the issue, sharing about people not knowing who they are or who He is for themselves. He shared how so many people really do not know Him, and live their lives vicariously through the preacher or another of their spiritual leaders, but they do not have a personal relationship with Him. He revealed how there are so many hurting people in the world, especially in the church, and how hurt people, out of their hurt, hurt people.

God revealed to me how many have unresolved deep hurts that they bring into relationships, and He reminded me how Pastor Boyer used to always say to me in counseling, "If you bury your pain alive, it will come out to hunt you in your future." God later revealed to me that's exactly what people do, they bury their pain deep within, convincing themselves they have dealt with it, when in fact they have not, and it comes up later at inopportune times, causing havoc in their lives.

I heard the Lord tell me in 2010 to get out; my marriage was over. I did not leave until 2017 after nearly losing my life twice, and receiving confirmation through my healthcare professionals, which I am sure rarely ever happens, but it did for me.

⌘

As I laid fighting for my life in the hospital with no insurance, the hospital, doing its due diligence to confirm actual insurance, after speaking to my husband and being told he had insurance, in the state he was living, that covered me, in their attempt to verify the information he provided them found no insurance. He insisted on several different occasions that he had insurance, which covered me, but the hospital was not able to verify.

After going back and forth with my husband several different times concerning this matter, the hospital representative told me she had checked thoroughly and had connections in the state my husband lived, and they had confirmed there was no insurance in place for him. The representative went on to tell me it was time for me to start making decisions and preparing for my own life, and they proceeded to assist me in getting assistance that was available for me here.

Then my Neurologist, a British doctor (remember I was given a specialist for all of my major organs due to the intense treatments I had to undergo) came into my room and said, "Mrs. Hunt do you mind if I ask you a personal question?" I gave him permission, and he proceeded to say, "You don't appear to be a promiscuous woman..."

I knew where the conversation was going, so I stopped him by responding, "You are correct; I have been with my husband for 33 years and have not been with any other man since becoming acquainted with him, but he to the contrary, has never been faithful to me." You would have thought I was related to this doctor as he became very upset; he looked at me and said, "I hope you divorced him," before leaving my room.

WOW, yeah reality set in hard, and I decided once I was well enough, I would obtain a divorce since we were living in separate states anyway, and my husband was not supporting me. There are so many things I have learned through this process; most importantly, it gave me the opportunity to seek God as to why people stay in bad, nonproductive relationships.

I have indeed learned so much. My entire life has been completely transformed, and I am ready to assist individuals who are in relationships, wanting to know how to make it better or be comfortable enough to leave it.

I survived by remaining faithful, no matter what my husband was doing, and understanding that what he was doing really had nothing to do with me, and everything to do with his own internal unresolved issues showing up and overtaking him.

I planted good seeds while in my marriage, seeds of Love, Joy, Peace, Patience, Kindness, Goodness, Faithfulness, Gentleness, and Self-Control, which are the nine fruits of the Spirit listed in the bible. I also sowed seeds of integrity, commitment, sacrifice, and I could go on and on.

Yes, I know now I should not have stayed so long, but there are lessons in that as well, which I have learned. I have planted good seeds, and I expect to reap a harvest in my next relationship. I will marry and live a life of bliss, filled with plenty of love and camaraderie that shows up in everything we do. It will be infectious to everything it touches, reaching the highest mountain while flowing through the lowest valleys changing everything it comes in contact with, in Jesus' name!

It is my sincere heartfelt prayer that every person who reads this Chapter be granted new insight into the possibilities of their current situations, and come to know personally that God really is no respecter of persons, understanding what He's done for me, He will do for YOU, and even greater things will He do because He loves YOU! "Won't He Do It... YES HE WILL!

SELF-REFLECTION

- So now, after reading this Chapter, what events in your life did you recall wherein you experienced operating in fear, causing you to self-sabotage? How did you handle it, and what if anything, would you do differently now?

- Have you ever had a time in your life when you thought something wasn't for you but in retrospect feel it could have been a divine set up tailor made for you? Share your thoughts.

- Think about opportunities you've had that you turned down out of fear. Are you encouraged to revisit them and request reconsideration?

Chapter 4

THE FIGHT TO RECONCILE
THE BROKEN PIECES

As I laid in bed daily, consuming a lot of pharmaceuticals for the continued treatment of Leukemia, I asked, "How do I begin again?" Every day I asked this question from the bottom of my heart, this was my sincere heartfelt prayer, "How do I begin again?" On one of those days after asking that question while holding my cell phone, a video popped up featuring John Hope Bryant speaking about Operation Hope, how befitting.

I listened intently; I was mesmerized by what he was sharing, his words infused me with hope, they spoke directly to my soul. Upon completion of the video, I contacted Operation Hope, and I was assigned to Joncey Lee, a Financial Wellbeing Coach for the organization.

I explained to Ms. Lee my physical condition at the time, but told her I was very interested in getting my life back on track and would greatly appreciate whatever assistance she could give me in building my finances and reconstructing my life. She provided me with all the paperwork I needed to get started in their program, and she began working with me in building my credit.

Ms. Lee was awesome as she sent me all the paperwork

via email. I printed the documents, completed them, scanned, and sent them back to her. All of our meetings were held over the telephone, so I didn't miss a beat, what an amazing experience, utilizing advance technology to get the job done. In fact, I would not meet Ms. Lee personally until a year later at another program I was participating in, wherein she was a Financial Literacy Presenter on behalf of Operation Hope.

❧

Ms. Lee pulled my credit report, went over it with me, and told me the things I had to address. She showed me how to dispute some issues, and we were off to the races. She met with me monthly via telephone to check the progress of her assignments to me. She later instructed me to open a secure credit card with the bank.

I went to the bank opened the secured credit card, and they also had a credit building program wherein they would give you a $1000 loan, you would put that money in a CD with them, and make monthly payments on the loan to rebuild your credit. Well, I took advantage of that as well.

My credit score started climbing, and I was excited! At the end of a year of making my credit card payments on time, the bank sent me a check for the amount I opened the secured credit card with, removed secure from my credit card, and added another $1000 credit limit on that card.

Yeah! I was on my way as my credit score had gone up by 100 points as well. I felt like I was making progress, I was doing the dang gone thing, and it felt amazing! I was truly grateful and very ecstatic, seeing how quickly my financial status was changing before my eyes. This was mind-blowing and awesome to me.

It was exactly what Mr. Bryant was talking about in his video wherein he said, "Nothing changes your life more than God and love than to move your credit score 120 points." I was experiencing what he was talking about within my first year of being in their program.

My obedience to working on my credit was divinely timed and rewarding. Unbeknownst to me was how soon I would have to use it, as my son and I discovered his roommate had decided to get married and, therefore, would not be renewing the lease to the apartment we were sharing.

Although my son made money, his credit score was tight due to student loan debt and high credit card balances, so when it came time for us to look for a place to live, we had no problems as my credit score was high enough for us to move and take advantage of all the perks available. We were able to successfully transition into our new place of choice in an amazing community with awesome amenities! "Won't He Do It… YES HE WILL!"

⁂

This accomplishment with Operation Hope's assistance manifested just in time for their 2018 Hope Global Forums Annual Meeting, which is known as the largest Financial Services Meeting in the world held here in Atlanta. I was asked to share my testimony on a conference call with some of their board members, which I did.

I was later contacted and asked if I would be willing to share before their 100-member Board of Directors prior to the official opening of the Forum. I shared what I have written herein before the Board of Directors, and there was not a dry eye in the room.

After leaving that meeting, I received a text asking would I be willing to share my testimony during the opening of the 2018 Hope Global Forum before over 1500 participants, I agreed. When I entered that auditorium filled with all those people and shining lights, it was electrifying; as I was escorted to the back to get on a mic before my turn to take the stage to share; I felt like a celebrity, it was so amazing!

After taking the stage and sharing my testimony in the presence of all those people, it became so real. Upon completion of my sharing, I was given a standing ovation! Whoa, my God, my God! As I left the stage, I had people greeting me and thanking me for sharing. Mr. Bryant himself told the crowd I was an emotional "Billionaire" as I left the stage, and I received that, oh yes, I did! I continued getting accolades throughout the event. I even met and took a picture with the one and only Chris Tucker! "Won't He Do It... YES HE WILL!"

❦

Well, that was great, but I still had work to do to get my life where I needed it to be, at a place where I am thriving and not merely surviving. I was indeed well on my way, but I was clear there was still work to be done on my part. As I continued to pray that prayer every day, what I needed showed up for me.

I heard the Lord say I had to get Certified as a Life Coach. I received information via email about the "Convergence Coach Certification" program. I really didn't want to do it as I felt it was too much at that time, so I asked God if I could do it the following year. I felt the price was high, and I just wasn't up to it at the time.

But how many of you know when God says something, and especially when He makes the way for it to happen as He did in this case, I had no choice but to be obedient and take the course. I took this course to become a Certified Life Coach, and it was a very intense, interactive course.

The material was deep content that dealt with the 3-dimensional person, mind, body, and soul of the individual. Not only did we have to digest all this material, but we also had to successfully coach a Pro Bono Client to complete the course. This was good, it required a lot, but it was well worth it, and I successfully completed the course and became a Certified Life Coach. Yes! "Won't He Do It… YES HE WILL!"

OMG, the next course that showed up for me in response to my prayer, of how do I began again, was entitled, "Freedom From Fear Forever." This course was truly life-changing. Prior to taking this course, no one could have told me fear was ruling my actions the way I discovered it was. I thought I was a Bold, Holy Ghost filled, Fire Baptized Sistah!

Well, I was, I just didn't realize my life was being led by the spirit of fear and this course began to expose it everywhere it was operating in my life. I could not believe what was happening to me through this course; I had powerful encounters with fear being exposed. This course took me through the process of bringing fear to the surface for elimination.

I discovered some deeply hidden fears in me that I had to release. The instructor for this course was a very anointed 'Woman of God' called to bring rhema word teachings to whosoever was interested in challenging their belief system and elevating to a higher level in Christ. I was amazed at how much this course opened me up to receive even deeper profound revelations from my Creator.

The next course that showed up for me was entitled, "Clearing The Way, Walking in Emotional and Spiritual FREEDOM." This course was perfect after experiencing Freedom From Fear Forever, as FFFF exposed deeply hidden fears and brought them to the surface for elimination, and Clearing the Way is the huge moving equipment that comes and takes it all away.

The lessons in this course were life-altering and extremely transformative. This course was taught by the same instructor for the Freedom From Fear Forever course, as well as the Convergence Coach Certification program, the one and only, Ericka D. James, CEO, Keynote Speaker, Trainer, and Prophetic Strategist, sent directly from heaven. OMG, you will never be the same after encountering her courses!

⌘

I was still in treatment for Leukemia during this time that I was taking all of these courses; I was determined to be ready to build my empire once I finished all treatments. I then heard the Lord tell me to take a course at my church, entitled "Master Teacher."

Now, this was entirely too much for me I didn't want to be called a "Master Teacher," as I really don't take titles lightly. "Master Teacher," why "Master Teacher?" Why not "Teacher?" That just hit my spirit too deep, plus this course was offered in the evenings, and I would have to walk to the train station, catch two trains, a bus, and then a cab to get to the class as I was not driving yet.

I really was not interested. Then I heard the Lord say, "You must take this class." Now, this was really interesting because I knew the Lord was going to do something out of the ordinary with me in this class, and sure enough, He did.

When it came to the final exam, we each had to do a presentation of our choosing. God had given me such a powerful presentation for my final that I had to offer a Disclaimer that read: ***"Please note, this is not a rebuke or belittling of The Holy Bible, so please keep an open mind. My assignment tonight in this final exam is to*** *create thought-provoking scenarios to assist in the opening of our Minds and Hearts to receive deeper revelations from God."*

My topic: "Biblical Thought-Provoking Conversation." My scripture reference: Romans 11:33, "Oh, the depth of the riches both of the wisdom and knowledge of God! How unsearchable are His judgments and His ways past finding out!" I began by asking the following questions:

- Who knew the interpretation of that verse without using any of the tools we use to interpret the verses of scripture?

- How can we know if this is what was intended to be written from the original scrolls from which it was allegedly taken?

- How many of us have seen the original scrolls from which the Holy Bible is supposedly interpreted?

Discussion ensued around the questions. Then the Lord had me to share what He had been revealing to me, how we are told the original languages of the scrolls of which the Holy Bible is conceived, are Greek and Hebrew. Yet, the Holy Bible, as we know it and read it, is in English. I posed the question, "Does anyone of us know exactly what it took to translate the scrolls into the English language, noting some words had to be substituted, as there were no matches for translation into the English language?"

With that said, the Lord had me share with them how

easy it is to mistranslate from English to English as the positioning of punctuation in a sentence in this language can completely change the entire meaning of the sentence. For example: "Let's eat, grandma" indicates we are inviting grandma to eat with us. However, remove the comma, and it reads, "Let's eat grandma," indicating grandma is the meal we are going to eat.

It's the same words simply remove the comma, and you have a completely different meaning. The Lord led me to share with them how using our class alone; we can start at the left side of the room, give a message to be share from each individual to the next until it reaches the last person on the right side of the room, and by the time the message arrives at the end, some words would have been lost and or changed, and the meaning of what was intended altered.

The Lord had me share while holding the Holy Bible in midair, "Contrary to popular belief about this book, much has been lost in translation, not to mention books that are missing." Moral of the lesson, the Lord wants us to know in order to be "Master Teachers," we must be at such a place spiritually with the True and Living God that we are able to receive revelation directly from Him, revealing the original intent and truth of the subject matter. We are responsible for receiving deep revelations from God and interpreting them to the masses as "Master Teachers," which is a heavy responsibility to carry and cannot be taken lightly.

When the Lord began revealing to me what He wanted me to share as my presentation for my final exam, I immediately asked Him how, and reminded Him that He would have to do it through me, as this was a tough discussion to have with the church for my final exam. As God would have it, all went well, and my lesson was embraced with love from everyone. Only God!

This is another of those lessons I won't share entirely here but will be using as I travel to share at various ministries around the world. Thank God I passed the course and received my Certificate! Who knows what impact this teaching had on the course itself. As I'm writing this, I'm reminded my Certificate doesn't say "Master Teacher," it reads "Teacher." To God be all the Glory for the things He does for me! God really does know the thoughts He has towards me, thoughts of good, not evil, to bring me to an expected end. God is not finished with me yet, "Won't He Do It… YES HE WILL!"

⚜

I can clearly see God is positioning me for His "Greater Works," as He is providing a lot of self-care development for me, as well as sharpening tools I'll need for the trade. The more I share, the more my eyes open to the things God has been saying to me all along; things that are becoming clearer through the process of writing this book.

My God has brought me through a lot, down a mighty long road to bring me to a predetermined expected end. I must pause here and do a praise dance! Hallelujah! If only you knew what I'm feeling right now. Tears are flowing down my cheeks as I write this. God is really good and so faithful. He chooses whom He will bless, and I am so glad God favors me! Hallelujah, thank you, Jesus, my God truly favors me! Just think, I always thought God favored everyone else, even while He was doing great things in my life, all I could see was how much He favored others, but not anymore! Thank you, Lord!

I wonder how many of you are like that, seeing only what God is doing in everyone else's life while neglecting to see what He is doing in your life. My God is no respecter of person; what He's done or does for one, He'll do for another just for the asking.

⚜

A friend of mine offered to pay for me to get my Health and Life Insurance License, so I took the Pre-License Study Course and passed the state exam for Health and Life Insurance Agent. This did indeed fit with my larger plan of providing financial services to the masses, teaching people how to create wealth. It reminded me of when the Lord spoke to me, saying, **"You will teach people how to create wealth from nothing."**

As I was still getting my treatments, things were coming together to help me get back on my feet. My heart's desire was to work in the Mortgage side of Real Estate, but you must be licensed as a Mortgage Loan Originator, and since that was my desire, I took the Pre-License Course to become licensed. This became one of the hardest endeavors of my life, as the Pre-License Course is a 20-hour course, then you sit for the state exam, but for me, this ran into an eight-plus month endeavor.

I failed the exam on my first attempt, and immediately afterwards had many obstacles present themselves to challenge me. Firstly, I lost my brother who was the first sibling to transition out of this realm. Secondly, before we could have his homegoing service, I lost my Aunt, my namesake, and Godmother. She was there assisting in the preparation of my brother's service, and she would not live to see it. This meant I would be out-of-state for a while through this process as they both resided in my hometown.

This time in my life was rough, as I was already feeling like things weren't coming together for me fast enough. While I saw a lot of accomplishments, I just felt my life was not coming together as fast as I would like. I had lost everything in my life; I was starting over at what I called ground zero, and I was getting a bit anxious.

I wanted to get back to work to prove to myself I was okay, and I was determined to work in the Mortgage Industry, but the test became my Jericho Wall. I would fail the test a second time, and I was so upset I was really thinking about throwing in the towel, but quitting was just not an option, nor was it a part of my makeup.

I was at a place where everything was on the line for me, as the rules of testing states, "If you fail this exam three consecutive times, you must wait six months before you would be allowed to take it again." I just didn't see myself being able to wait six more months if I failed again, so yes, everything was on the line for me. I just kept studying and preparing myself; I didn't know what else to do.

As I studied and prayed, time was passing me by and before you know it, I looked up, and the month I was scheduled to go to Costa Rica was upon me. I felt the pressure as I had not yet passed this exam, nor had I gotten everything I needed to be ready to go on this trip. The first thing I did was schedule my exam, and it so happened I scheduled it the Sunday before the Wednesday I was to leave on my trip.

Well, I know it was nobody but God, as I had no intention of taking this test this close to my trip, but before I knew it, I had hit the buttons on the computer and scheduled the exam. Well, I said, "This is it; I must do it." I really wanted to reschedule the test, but I just couldn't. I felt the time had come for this Jericho Wall to fall once and for all!

<hr />

SELF-REFLECTION

- Do you recall a time in your life wherein a crisis presented you with an opportunity as described at the beginning of this chapter? Describe.

- What do you think about the distance and method traveled to take the "Master Teachers" class? Have you ever had to take as many different modes of transportation just to take a class you did not want to take in the first place?

- How about the 20-hour course plus state exam which took over eight months to accomplish, what, if any, incidents have you had like that in your life? Explain.

"I can do all things through Christ which strengtheneth me."

(Philippians 4:13)

Chapter 5

MY JOURNEY TO COSTA RICA

I would never have thought my first trip out of the country would be to Costa Rica. I thought it would be to Africa the love of my life, but it really was to Costa Rica. In this Chapter, I will share with you the things that transpired to make this trip a reality.

My hope is to help you see there really are divine synchronicity of events happening in our lives daily. This was an amazing experience, and I could clearly see a system of things at work on my behalf to make my trip possible. So, fasten your seatbelt and take this ride with me as I share my journey to the exquisite Costa Rica, my first experience out of the country!

My journey to Costa Rica began with an email I received in May 2018 from my Life Coach/Therapist, Melissa Edwards Brown, announcing a "Next Level" expedition to Costa Rica. The more I read the email, and I read it many times, the more I began feeling deep down in my soul the need to say yes to this adventure, exploration, and excavation of self.

The email spoke of preparing for the "Next Level" of your life; everything in the email was very intentional and spoke directly to my soul. With All I had come through over the last four years alone made me feel, even more, the need to say "Yes" to me, putting me first for the first time in my life!

I felt this trip would be a renewing of my soul, and would nourish me in ways I didn't know I needed nourishing. I just knew this trip would delve into the marrow of my being, and totally transform me.

The trip was scheduled for October 31st – November 4th. Although I was still recovering from major illnesses and was not yet working, I had no doubt I would be back to work and able to meet the payment plan the Host offered for this journey, and have whatever finances I would need to enjoy the trip.

As God would have it, I was able to pay for my trip by the August 31st deadline. I was ecstatic that the way had been made for me to pay off my trip to Costa Rica; I was beyond excited! This is a good place to explain the wonder of how I was able to pay for my trip.

As my desire was great to be a part of this adventure, I heard the Lord speak to me and say, **"You keep saying how much you want to go on this trip, but you haven't even clicked on the button within the email to find out what is required for the trip."**

So, I opened the email again for the millionth time and clicked on the button showing the details, and it took me directly to PayPal, requesting a $250.00 non-refundable deposit. I thought for a moment, *umm, I know PayPal would allow me to order merchandise and give me two weeks to pay for it, but,* I thought, *two weeks is not enough time for me to pay for this trip.*

Then I noticed that they offered credit, I hesitated, because I really didn't want to apply for any more credit. But, before I knew it, I had completed the credit application, and within seconds PayPal had extended me a line of credit which paid for my trip. And they allowed me to take advantage of their promotion that would give me six months interest-free on the repayment. WOW, I said this was surely my confirmation I was supposed to be on this trip! "Won't He Do It... YES HE WILL!"

⚜

I was focused and determined to get back to work, and my interest was to be a Mortgage Loan Originator. I had taken the Pre-License Course and even sat for the state exam unsuccessfully by the time I got the email announcement of the expedition. However, I was confident I would be working, and my finances would be okay for me to thoroughly enjoy this trip. I sat for the exam a second time unsuccessfully.

Now, I was really concerned, as noted in the last Chapter, I would be required to wait six-months if I failed a third time. I really took my studying seriously, but I just couldn't figure out what I didn't know. I didn't feel the test was hard at all, and yet I had failed it twice. In the meantime, many distractions hit me. I had lost my brother and my aunt. I just felt like I couldn't get a break. While I was distracted by these events, time was passing by.

The more I re-read the announcement for this trip, I had no doubt it was for me, I didn't know how I would do it, but I knew this trip was for me. There was a section in the email that read, **"The truth is there is a brilliance deep within you. You are a creative genius. No one can do what you do, like you do. You are gifted beyond belief, full of ideas, strategy, resources, and wisdom. In so many ways, you've been a hidden jewel, the best-kept secret. But how long are you going to use what God gave you to build up everyone else's dream? How long are you going to create success for other people, while you struggle and settle for a side hustle for yourself? It's time to stop hiding and go all in."**

Oh My God! Talk about being convicted, this message reminded me of what the Lord had spoken to me late one night a couple of years ago. He said, **"I did not give you gifts and talents for you to use to feed everyone else while you starve."** If that wasn't enough, it also reminded me of a time I was in a business meeting, and I was praising and supporting a friend in the business when Bishop Charles Carroll came to me and said, **"Be careful always being a cheerleader for everyone, and focus on doing the business, or else you will look up one day and find that you have become simply a cheerleader for everyone else."** WOW, a double whammy, so I knew this trip was calling my name SUPER LOUD!

I began hearing in the spirit how there was going to be an unusual and uncommon favor of God upon this trip, so I immediately shared it with the Host. After hearing this, it never dawned on me that I personally would experience unusual and uncommon favor.

Yet, as I now look over the events leading up to and through my going on this trip, I realize God was revealing to me that I would experience unusual and uncommon favor. It is clearly the only reason I was able to go to Costa Rica. It is amazing how we are forewarned about events concerning our lives and how easily we overlook it thinking it's for everyone else, sometimes never recognizing that a message through you is always for you first.

My Spirit man begin leaping at the thought of the trip. I felt so extremely excited about the mentioning of it, but still, I did not have the finances for my passport and flight. So, during the months following my final payment, I remained in faith that God would make a way for me to get my passport and flight. I spent a lot of that time completing job readiness training classes, trying to get back to work, to no avail.

I really thought I would be working and able to get my passport and flight with ease. Eight months had passed, and I had not yet passed the state Mortgage Loan Originator's exam, and that's where a lot of my focus was through the process of this journey to getting to my trip. With my focus and attention being on the exam, time passed by, and before I knew it, the week of the trip was upon me.

It was Sunday, October 28th, I had scheduled myself to sit for the Mortgage Loan Originator's test. This was peculiar to me because I was aware this was the week of my trip, and I really didn't want the pressure of taking this test on me. I thought about scheduling it for the week after my trip, but before I knew it, I had scheduled it. This would be my third attempt, everything was on the line as I wanted to get in the Mortgage business, but this state exam was standing between me and that desire.

Although I was scheduled for the exam, I felt like I was still missing something. I knew I had faithfully studied my material, but I felt like I still had not connected the dots. Well, a very special young man I befriended earlier this year, unbeknownst to what I was feeling, was led to send me a link to NMLS approved Mortgage training videos.

Now get this everyone, this young man whose name is: Wajutome Goodluck Obriko, lives all the way in Nigeria, Africa. I need you to see how God will use whoever avails himself to get His children what they need at any given time. God is not bound by time, space, distance or anything else. I am still amazed at how this young man knew exactly what to send to me. I know it was nobody but God, as time was of the essence.

This was just a couple of days before my scheduled exam. When I tell you the training he sent me was indeed God sent. It was perfect, and the instructor was very much an anointed teacher from heaven, an Angel. Through her method of teaching, I was able to compartmentalize all the information I had taken from my earlier studies. I was finally able to connect the dots; I could clearly understand how and where the pieces of information in my head fit on the exam. It was amazing, "Won't He Do It... YES HE WILL!"

***

Well, on Sunday, October 28th, I, Joyce R. Rogers, finally successfully passed the state exam. Hallelujah! I cannot express how elated I was for this accomplishment. I began to think about how amazing it was for me to have passed this exam three days before my scheduled trip to Coast Rica. The thoughts began flooding my mind of how perfectly timed this was and how awesome it would be to go on this trip on the cusps of such a great accomplishment for me after all I had been through. Yet I didn't have two pennies to rub together, and I still did not have my passport or flight.

Monday morning arrives! It was now October 29th, two days before the departure of my sisters headed to Costa Rica. I was on my morning prayer call when one of the prayer warriors, unaware of my dilemma, was led by the Spirit of God to share her testimony of how she posted a prayer request with a picture of her passport on her window wherein she declared she would like to take a trip out of the country before the end of 2018.

She explained that shortly thereafter, she received a call from a girlfriend of hers asking her if she wanted to take an all-expense-paid trip with her to Mexico, noting the only thing required of her was to supply her own food. WOW! "Won't He Do It... YES HE WILL!"

Her testimony ignited my flicker of faith, and I begin to praise God for what He did for her while reminding Him how He was no respecter of persons, what He did for my sister He could do for me. I begin to declare that God could indeed make a way out of no way for me to get my passport, and my roundtrip flight paid for in time for me to make it on my trip to Costa Rica, which was two days away. Another thing the sister shared on the prayer line was how she stayed ready with her luggage packed to go.

I quickly realized that I wanted to go on this trip, but I had not done anything in the natural to demonstrate my faith in going, so I called my sistah-friend, Denise Rivers, and asked her if she could run me to J.C. Penney to pick up a few things. This loving soul of a sistah immediately agreed. Now, I want you to understand the depth of what's happening here, so picture in your mind's eye that this sister lives south of Georgia approximately 30-40 minutes away, which could very easily turn into an hour, or an hour and a half long drive just to get to me due to the traffic here. Still, she was indeed willing to do it for me, and she did.

I must also say, she traveled that distance to take me to the Mall that was about 15 minutes away from me, and she clearly understood how horrible the traffic gets here, but she was willing to do it for me, no questions asked. Please keep in mind that I didn't have two pennies to rub together, as the old folks use to say, nor did I have my passport or flight tickets at this point.

At the time sister Rivers agreed to do this for me, she

was not at all aware of what was going on, hint, hint, she demonstrated agape love and what true friendship looks like. She knew me and understood that if I asked her, it was of importance. I would like to pause here and add that when you are flowing in the spirit and truly connected in sisterhood, there's no need for a bunch of questions. When a sister requests your help, you simply show up.

When sister Rivers arrived, she noticed I lived near a Mall within walking distance. I explained to her that J.C. Penney was not located in that Mall, and since I didn't have any cash, I was using my J.C. Penney credit card. We both could not believe J.C. Penney wasn't located within that Mall, and we got a good laugh as for a split second, she thought it odd for me to call her knowing the distance she had to travel to reach me when I was within walking distance of a Mall. I wanted to share this, so you could see the human side of us even when we're walking in the spirit. She was led by the Spirit to come without questions, but after seeing a Mall close to me, her humanist side showed up!

On our journey to the Mall I explained to her what was going on and how I had just allowed someone to borrow my luggage. I told her how my faith had been ignited by the testimony of a sister on my prayer line earlier that morning, and I shared the testimony with her. I then shared with her how I had paid for a trip to Costa Rica, which was scheduled to begin in two days, and how I didn't have my passport or flight tickets to make the trip.

Then her faith was ignited, and she shifted into a faith

mode that agreed with mine, believing that I should indeed make this trip. Hence, she provided part of the cash for my passport. My awesome prayer line host, Cynthia Harper, provided the rest that I needed to pay for my passport. So, I was able to keep my appointment, which I had scheduled by faith for Tuesday, October 30th, to get my passport after having rescheduled it twice due to lack of funds. "Won't He Do It... YES HE WILL!

So here arrives Tuesday, October 30th, the day before my scheduled trip, I arrive at the place to get my passport, only to find after submitting all my supporting documents I would have to come back after 2:00pm to pick it up! So, I'm there, and I finally get my passport in hand. "WOW," I exclaim, "I am one step closer!" My sisters were all scheduled to leave the next day, headed for Costa Rica, and I still didn't have my plane ticket.

My luggage was now packed and sitting at the door since the day before I received my passport, as an act of faith. After hearing my sister's testimony on that prayer call, it caused me to stand up in faith and begin to do things in the natural that demonstrated my faith that what I needed would materialize. My calling sister Rivers to take me to the Mall to purchase my luggage and packing it, further blew oxygen on my faith flame and caused heaven to respond by touching others to assist in making this trip a reality for me.

I was led by God to post in our prayer line messenger group that I was short and in need of some help to purchase my flight to make this trip. I asked if anyone could loan me the amount I needed or if multiple people could do a smaller amount to help me. Well before I knew it my prayer team swung into action further fanning the flame of faith.

One person sent me $11.11, and man did that ignite my faith even more and sparked a revelation within me of how simple life would be if we all gave a little of what we have to those in need how much better our world would be, and that number reminded me my Angels are working it out for me. Then another sister gave $50, and two other sisters joined together and gave $40. WOW, before I knew it, I had what I needed to get my plane ticket! I received exactly what I needed to get my flight tickets. Oh My God! "Won't He Do It... YES HE WILL!"

Howbeit, I just missed being able to get the late flight out on the day of the trip, which was Wednesday, October 31st, so I had to get the next flight on Thursday, November 1st, at 6:00pm, putting me at the resort around midnight or later. No problem, I secured the flight.

This meant I would miss two days and one night of my trip, but it did not matter to me, as I knew I had to be there, and no matter when I arrived, it would be exactly the time I was supposed to be there. Here it was, Tuesday evening, the night before my sisters would all be flying out to Costa Rica, and I now had both my passport and my roundtrip plane tickets.

While resting in a state of gratitude, thanking God, and

communing with Him, I, out of a grateful heart, decided to ask God why He liked working at the eleventh hour? Informing Him how I didn't like that, noting I am proactive in being prepared for things, but my experience with Him is He loves coming through at the eleventh hour. Well, as God would have it, He kindly breathed on me His breath of life again and allowed me to feel a long soft breeze of fresh warm air across my face as He responded to my temporary state of ignorance. The following is His response to me:

"It's not that I like to wait until the eleventh hour to give you something, it is because of you that you don't see or receive it until after the eleventh hour. Out of fear, doubt, and unbelief, you wander around distracted by every wind and wave thinking <u>DOING</u> is going to somehow produce it. You don't recognize that you're being distracted, and therefore, neglect to be <u>STILL and UNMOVED</u> in my presence to receive My instructions about the matter. I provide the answers upon request, as I did with Daniel, and your enemy is YOU not being disciplined to receive the answer. It is not until the eleventh hour that YOU finally make yourself be still and earnestly seek me for the answer. Stop asking me for a miracle and then moving forward with your plans as to how it should manifest. The key is after making your request known to me, BE STILL in My presence, and I shall answer."

Well, needless to say, He put me in my place! This was such revelation to me, as before this revealing, I always told people God loves working in the eleventh hour; so now guess who won't be telling anyone that anymore!

The next day sister Rivers and I were talking and praying. We asked God about how was it we could have so much knowledge of Him and relationship with Him, yet there are times in our lives when regardless of what we know or how much He uses us or how many miracles He has performed on our behalf, that we still find ourselves stuck and overwhelmed because we don't see what we need manifesting at any given time. So, we began questioning God about the reason behind it. He revealed the following to me the next day during my meditation:

"Daughter, you find yourselves in that place because you continue to live life as if YOU must DO and BE everything in making things happen in your life. The Body of Christ must understand there is a divine reason for each part, and each part has its separate and unique function. I've established that each part connects perfectly for supplying the other so as to be able to function as a WHOLE. As with the physical body, so likewise with my chosen body. Daughter, you have not been connected to your other parts so as to be able to be supplied so you can function on a greater plane of manifestation. I have a complete order and system of operating, and within My established system, I don't have anything dependent upon itself. Everything and Everyone has a part to play in the greater fulfillment and manifestation of the

things to come. Case-in-point: I used Moses, my servant, mightily and spoke to him personally on many occasions, yet I did not speak to Him personally to inform him of the need to use wisdom in delegating responsibilities to not overwhelm himself. I used Jethro his Father-In-Law to travel from a foreign country to tell him he must delegate the workload so as to allow for the manifestation of the greater work and to prevent him from possibly destroying himself. I have anointed and appointed people for different assignments, and my people must come quickly into the true revelation of what I mean when I say each joint supply the other."

My, my, this is deep revelation right here!!! This knocked me for a loop, and I had to pause for the rest of the day before continuing, so please should you find the need to pause, here would be a good place to do it. I could see what was being revealed here, so much can be gleaned from what is shared. It reminded me of an experience I had in Costa Rica, wherein this revelation was manifested before my very eyes. I will cover this in detail in the next Chapter.

❦

Finally, Thursday, November 1st, my departure to Costa Rica, I arrive at the airport, and stop at the curbside check-in to check my luggage. After loading my one large piece of luggage on the scale, the representative said, "Your luggage is overweight, that will be $168.00, please." After gathering my composure from the shock of this information, I replied, "Sir, I don't have $168.00."

He kindly stepped away for a moment and returned with this large paper bag. He handed it to me and said, "Take some of your clothes out and put in there and carry it on the airplane." I commenced unloading my luggage and carrying the extras onto the plane with me, as a carry-on. This was more of God's unusual and uncommon favor being shown to me. WOW, saved by GRACE, my God is good! "Won't He Do It... YES HE WILL!"

So herein you have shared in my journey to Costa Rica, now prepare yourselves as I take you into my experiences while there. Hold tight, it gets better and better! I'll meet you in the next Chapter.

SELF-REFLECTION

- What do you think about not having a passport or flight tickets two days before the trip? Have you experienced situations like this? What were your results?

- Can you recall a time when your faith was ignited in this manner? Will you explain what happened?

- Share your perspective on this Chapter?

Chapter 6

MY EXPERIENCE IN THE EXQUISITE COSTA RICA: THE MINI GARDEN OF EDEN, AN ILLUSTRIOUS PARADISE

I enjoyed my non-stop evening flight on Delta airlines from Georgia to the lovely Costa Rica; it was a smooth flight with minimal turbulence. They served food, drinks, and provided free movies on my flight, talk about the royal treatment. Oh my God, let me pause here and do a praise dance! I felt amazing, I was alone, and it was awesome to walk through the airport, get through Customs with ease to discover a driver holding a sign with my name on it awaiting me!

WOW, did I feel important! I had a private escort from the airport to the Tabacon Thermal Resort & Spa, which was almost three hours away from the airport, beautifully nestled high in the mountains of Costa Rica. What an awesome excursion it was and a truly amazing way to begin my experience in Costa Rica! I must admit, I didn't even realize the effects of all this until I started writing this chapter, and it is blowing my mind all over again. WOW!

The driver was very polite and attentive to my needs, offering me water and making sure my seat was positioned correctly for the long ride and inquiring if I wanted to stop somewhere to get something to eat. He went out of his way to ensure I was comfortable, including providing me with

Wi-Fi connection and allowing me to charge my cell phone. He and I had a wonderful time conversing, he shared with me a lot of the history and culture there.

He explained there was zero percent pollution! What!... that was the first impressive piece of information he provided me. He then shared how the Government got rid of its Military base and elected to reinvest the monies spent on the Military base into its people, land, and environment. WOW, that was the second most impressive thing he shared! Although it was dark, I could see some of the amazing trees that lined the roadway.

There were all sorts of trees lining the roadway up the mountain, trees I had never seen before. This road trip to the resort was wonderfully amazing, I told the driver his driving was putting me to sleep, as there were many winding roads going up the mountain, and I felt like a baby in a cradle, being rocked to sleep. While it was a very soothing ride, I never went to sleep from all the conversing between the driver and I.

❧❦❧

Upon arriving at the resort, I was immediately impressed with the natural aroma of the air. It was breathtaking; I had never experienced anything like it before unless I was giving myself aromatherapy, and even with that, my aroma therapies could not touch what I was experiencing. This was the natural atmosphere at the Tabacon Thermal Resort & Spa, fresh aromas in the air from the beautiful plant life surrounding it. The amazing plants that lined this resort left you awestruck.

I couldn't believe the natural colors I was observing, and I could see this beauty at night upon my arrival, so I could only imagine what I was in store for at sunrise. The thoughts began to flood my mind; I wondered if I had come on the first day with everyone else, would I have noticed or experienced all that I've described herein. This is my proof that this trip was personally designed just for me. This represented more of the unusual and uncommon favor that was revealed to come in the last chapter. Look at God! Won't He Do It… YES HE WILL!

Finally, I was all checked in, and while awaiting my escort to my room, I was provided with a freshly prepared fruit drink that was out of this world. It was made with lemons and cucumbers, and God only knows what else, it was so refreshing and extremely tasty. Now keep in mind, I arrived after midnight, and they still provided me with this delectable freshly made drink. Again, what Royal treatment I was experiencing. This was like being in paradise here on earth!

My escort arrives, loads my luggage and myself onto a very nice golf cart, and proceeds to take me to my room. It was so amazing, breathing in such fresh aromas and seeing the awesome landscape throughout the ride to my room. I arrived at my room, and was let in by my escort, who also took my luggage into my room. I was immediately impressed with the size of the room.

The commotion of my arrival awakened my roommate, who was just as excited to see me as I was to see her. We greeted one another with hugs and kisses. She began to give me a complete tour of our room. My roommate's name was Jenee from California, a spirited sister I met at a woman's gathering in Seattle, Washington, a couple of years prior. When I discovered she was coming on this trip to Costa Rica, I felt strongly she would be my roommate, and so she was.

While the hour was late and we had an early morning, she and I couldn't resist taking this opportunity to sit and catch up on what had been happening in our lives. Oh, what sisterhood. We laughed and cried, sharing so many things. It was like we were having our very own personal slumber party!

God used her to expound and express some important things to me, and likewise, He used me to do the same for her. It was truly amazing camaraderie between us, even thou we had spent so little time together since we first met. The hour had gotten very late, and we both decided it was time for us to go to sleep, as we were scheduled to meet the other sisters in the lobby to load onto our tour bus by 8:00am to begin the festivities of the day.

We arose early in the morning after a very late night, feeling renewed and energized for what was prepared for us this new day, my first, her third, nevertheless, we were ready. We got up early enough to have breakfast. Now, this being my first day of daylight, Jenee showed me patio doors, which led to the outside of our room. Oh my God, extremely breathtaking! The landscape was out of this world, tall plants, short plants, very bright colored plants, light-colored plants, you name it. The aroma was to live for. Beautiful stones lined our doorway, and you could see the Volcano. Every yard was lined with tall plants, providing privacy. There was a walkway also lined with tall, brilliant flowing, bright-colored plants behind our room, leading to other areas of the resort; it was simply magnificent!

Jenee and I made it to the breakfast buffet where we saw some of our sisters. We sat and had some more wonderful fellowship while enjoying the freshly prepared foods. The restaurant was elegant and very open to nature, a real open-air restaurant. Again, the breathtaking natural aromas filled the atmosphere. The sounds of nature were electrifying; we could hear birds chirping, woodpeckers pecking, water flowing, and God only knows the other sounds we heard, as we sat and enjoyed our lovely meal surrounded by such exquisiteness.

Well, the time had arrived for us to meet in the front lobby to board our tour bus, so we all commenced heading toward the lobby. After boarding the bus, our tour guide did a headcount and discovered there was one more above the number he had for participants, so he was informed I was a late arrival. He suggested I wait until after the tour and be sure to go to the tour office to let them know. He proceeded to explain the adventures planned for the day. He informed us we would be going for a hike through the Rainforest, and from there, we would go over to the waterfall a short distance away. I don't know if any of us were really prepared for a hike through the Rainforest, as he so subtly announced, but we were all in.

As we arrived at the Rainforest, we freshened up, and some took pictures. We all were amazed at the awesome view. It was such a beautiful site to see! It was so unassuming; you couldn't tell from the entrance what you were about to experience. When you think Rainforest, your mind tends to stir up emotions or pictures about too many insects and animals of all sorts. I want you to know if you have never visited a Rainforest, you will be absolutely amazed at the beauty and harmony of life within it.

We began down the trail with our tour guide teaching us about the various trees and different birds that showed up. Our minds and attention were fixated on every word of the tour guide, as we were being led into the Forest. The environment was so open, at this point, you didn't think about a forest; you simply followed the tour guide as he continuously explained the meaning of practically everything we passed. He led us over to a mini waterfall, wherein he explained how the frogs come there to lay their eggs on the branches of the trees above the waterfall so that they would fall into the water and develop, and that's how they have their humble beginnings. It was truly amazing to hear, and a beautiful site to see.

He led us further into what we could now see was the Forest, showing us holes in the earth where Tarantulas lived.

He shined the flashlight into the hole so we could see inside, and he explained their purpose and what they were doing. We almost passed a poisonous snake camouflaged on a tree limb, which he pointed out to us and explained how that snake would stay on that tree limb for about 7-9 days until his food, certain insects, flew to him, and he would then feed before moving on. This information reminded me of how God had revealed to me the importance of knowing the time and era in which we live. Watching this snake and hearing its process reminded me of when God told me the old paradigm was one of working hard by the sweat of our brow. He explained to me how we have now entered His new paradigm of the "Suddenly" and having our desires manifest effortlessly! This snake lies and waits for his food to come to him. Wow! What better example of "effortless" do we need? I know this might be a bit hard to receive, as we have been trained to work hard for what we want, but I believe God. If He said it, that settles it!

As we walked the trail at various times, our tour guide would stop abruptly, and we didn't know if we should run for cover or what. He would calm us and explain that he heard a certain sound, and he would point in the direction of the sound and explain to us what animal he heard and what the sound represented. This freaked us out the first couple of times it happened, but then it began to mesmerize us whenever he did it, as we saw firsthand how in tune he was with nature. It was awesome to witness such attunement with creation.

As we got further into the Forest after explaining about the purpose of so many different species of animals and trees, we came upon a bat cave. Seeing the fear in some of the participants, he asked us what we believed was the most dangerous animal or insect to humans. We all gave our opinions of what we thought was the most dangerous to man, and he kindly informed us it was the mosquito and shared with us how the mosquito is killing people more than any other animal or insect in the world. He went on to ask us what we thought was the greatest threat to the mosquito. He politely informed us it was the bat, noting our fears of them are somewhat linked to the myth of Dracula. This new information had us all looking at the importance of bats and our fear of them a little differently now.

He went on to explain how everything has a purpose, noting with all the various life forms within the Forest, everything has a purpose, and it all works together in harmony to sustain life within the Forest. Again, his teaching provoked a revelation in me about how God created everything to work in harmony with one another and reminded me of what God spoke to me that I shared in chapter 5, but believe it bears repeating here, as a reminder and perhaps greater clarity: **"Daughter, you find yourselves in that place because you continue to live life as if YOU must DO and BE everything in making things happen in your life. The Body of Christ must understand there is a divine reason for each part, and each part has its separate and unique function. I've established that each part connects perfectly for** supplying the other so as to be able to function as a **WHOLE. As with the physical body, so likewise with my chosen body. Daughter, you have not been connected to your other parts so as to be able to be supplied so you can function on a greater plane of manifestation. I have a complete order and system of operating, and within My established system, I don't have anything dependent upon itself. Everything and Everyone has a part to play in the greater fulfillment and manifestation of the things to come. Case-in-point: I used Moses, my servant, mightily and spoke to him personally on many occasions, yet I did not speak to Him personally to inform him of the need to use wisdom in delegating responsibilities to not overwhelm himself. I used Jethro his Father-In-Law to travel from a foreign country to tell him he must delegate the workload so as to allow for the manifestation of the greater work and to prevent him from possibly destroying himself. I have anointed and appointed people for different assignments, and my people must come quickly into the true revelation of what I mean when I say each joint supply the other."** WOW, can you feel the dots being connected here?

The tour guide then talked about the workings of creation at ground level in the Forest and how there is a whole lot going on daily at that level. He posed another question to us, asking what we thought was the number one thing all of creation in the Forest is vying for at ground level. Again, we all gave our opinions, and he informed us it was "light." He further explained that because of so many trees in the Forest, there's very little light at ground level.

He then instructed us to look up, and wow, what beauty we beheld as we saw how tall the trees were, but we also saw one tree from ground level looking specifically like a big bunch of broccoli, so amazing to see as we looked up. Nevertheless, we saw the openness of space and all the sunlight at the top, to his point. He went on to share how everything needed for living was at that level as well, with fewer things vying for its attention, explaining the higher you go in the Forest, the less you are concerned about vying for sunlight.

Whoa, whoa! I can't speak for anyone else, but this journey through the Rainforest sure did speak to my soul. All I could hear was this is true of life; the higher you go in life, the fewer people you encounter vying to take you out for a position! WOW, there were so many life lessons as we hiked through this amazing paradise of a garden. As we moved on, we found ourselves at the first suspension bridge. I remember all the times I saw videos of people walking across these bridges, and I always thought those people must be crazy to walk across a bridge, suspended in mid-air, that sways as you move across it. Yet here I was faced with my chance to challenge my fears of height, experiencing the unknown, and being in mid-air without a body harness of some type.

To my great surprise, I took on the challenge and walked across this amazing bridge, high above everything.

Remembering when we were at ground level looking up, realizing we were now above what we just moments earlier found ourselves looking up at, which brings me to another life lesson. As long as you continue to move forward in life, you will find yourself above what you once felt was overwhelming you.

We were now looking down on the top of the trees, which we had been looking up at in amazement a short time earlier. There was a clearer view of the Volcano, and the scenery was simply breathtaking. I had no fear. I was so intrigued by what I was experiencing, I felt such a freedom being up so high above everything. There was such a rush of adrenaline through me that I don't think I was really aware of what I had accomplished until after it was all over.

It wasn't until I got home that I got the revelation I had walked up to that suspension bridge. While at home sitting on my bed, I heard God ask, "Joyce, how did you get to the suspension bridge? There were no elevators there." BAM, I suddenly realized I had walked up to the highest elevated suspension bridge in Costa Rica and crossed over it! You have to understand why this was so important to me, as just a year ago, I could not peddle five minutes on an Elliptical or Bike. My God, with that realization, my mind was thoroughly blown! I also realized how much I had counted myself out of a lot of things in life without ever attempting them.

I began to think about all the things I said I couldn't or wouldn't do without ever trying them, and it simply blew my mind! This revelation filled me with such hope of me moving forward through life, courageously trying, and experiencing new things, especially things I had said no to in the past without trying. I wonder how many things you have counted yourself out of without attempting them, saying you can't do this, or you can't do that, and you don't like this, or you don't like that.

My life will never be the same because of my experiences in Costa Rica. This trip has indeed, truly changed my perspective of my life. My trip across that suspension bridge delved deep into the marrow of my soul and made me feel so enlightened, transformed, and electrified while at the same time causing me to feel invigorated! I pray you get the picture; it was very much a life-changing experience for me.

Little did we know we had reached the height of our lessons through the majestic Rainforest, and the crossing of that suspension bridge was the beginning of our descent back to our starting point of this divine journey through the Rainforest. As we journeyed down, we crossed over multiple suspension bridges en route back to our humble beginnings of this miraculous tour, and with each bridge, I became freer and freer and freer. By the time I reached the bottom, I was new and transformed. You couldn't tell me I can't conquer the world; I was ready for anything now.

As we loaded back on our tour bus, the decision was made to have lunch before going to the waterfall, as we were not expecting the tour through the Rainforest to be so long. As we left the Rainforest, the bus driver stopped in the middle of the road, another one of those experiences we had become accustomed to in the Rainforest with our tour guide.

He stopped and said something to the tour guide, and the tour guide and his understudy grabbed their equipment and proceeded to get off the bus. Once outside, they set up their equipment and called everyone off the bus to see. As we each looked through the telescope, we could see this truly amazing bright colored toucan bird within a tree. After each one of us looked at the bird, we all marveled at how the bus driver could spot that bird when we couldn't see it without the help of the telescope.

Again, it was another truly amazing demonstration of how in tune the natives are with nature. It was an awesome thing to see, to witness how mankind could live in harmony with nature and everyone be happy, which brings me to another observation about Costa Rica. The air was so pristine that there was no fear or anxiety in the air at all, even the dogs were friendly and free without leashes, walking in the roadway, confident they would not be hit and coming up to people calmly to greet them.

This reminded me of how back at our rooms there was a raccoon family, yes, I said raccoon, that would come out amongst the people like they were a part of the family. There was no fear of them, and the natives explained they did not have any rabies there. It was truly amazing to witness! Everything about the atmosphere was very calming, there was no rushing around or busyness to get things done; it was a very calm and relaxed atmosphere.

We arrived at the second gorgeous open-air restaurant; this was not the one we ate breakfast at earlier; nevertheless, it was just as stunning. The gardens that surrounded this one was breathtaking but uniquely different. On one side, they had the area where they grew their vegetables and herbs used in preparing fresh meals. When you looked to the opposite side, you saw the different colored plant life.

You could see the birds enjoying the plants, and hear the hummingbirds enjoying their environment, even the birds were amazingly colorful. The environment was so beautiful to the eyes! The centerpieces on the tables sparked a lot of table discussion as to whether they were real or fake flowers. They were so colorful to the eye they looked fake.

However, after further discussion, we all realized, seeing the various colorful flowers growing all around the restaurant as well as the entire resort, we concluded there was no way they could be fake. Then we did the feel and smell test to confirm they were real. Some of those flowers looked like the fake wax flowers we would purchase back home, but these were the real deal.

The food was out of this world tasty; they prepare everything fresh, all their ingredients are freshly grown, even their meats, and they use no preservatives. You could really taste the difference. Everyone in our group was impressed with the tenderness of their meats and the overall flavor of the food. While we were eating, they did a demonstration of the making of their coffee using Costa Rica's famous coffee beans, and they allowed the coffee drinkers in our group to partake. Those who participated felt there was a difference in the taste from what they were accustomed to drinking.

After enjoying such an exquisite meal, our tour guide informed us he had a surprise for us and invited us to walk a short path to what he called the barn area. It was a very nice and cozy open-air space beside the restaurant, where it looked like you could have a barn fire and enjoy your evening out. Well, the tour guide seated everyone, and then he did a demonstration of how they take the natural sugar cane and juice it through a hand-operated machine. He handed everyone a shot glass and proceeded to pour everyone some of the sugar cane juice.

WOW, to my amazement, it was a very tasty drink. I thought it was going to be too sweet to drink like that, but it really was not. It was a great drink in its natural form. Then he pulled out his home-made bottle of what we would call Vodka in our country and proceeded to fill the glasses for a toast. I was too chicken to try it, so I opted to have a refill of the sugar cane juice for the toast. It was a nice surprise and very thoughtful of him to give us such a moving surprise in the cozy setting of the open-air barn.

We had the best tour guide in Costa Rica as I remember when we were going through the Rainforest, how other groups were speeding by us as our tour guide was explaining details to us about the Forest. We were so blessed; it bears to witness that our tour guide was another example of unusual and uncommon favor from God!

Well, as life would have it, once you've learned one life lesson and get to a place of growth, your next challenge will always present itself, and this time was no different. As we loaded back on our tour bus for the next journey, we were all told we were now going over to the waterfall. It was at this point that we were told there was a location there where we could watch the waterfall without going to its base, or we could travel to the base of the waterfall, but to get there, we would have to climb down "500 steps."

As I sat during the ride to the waterfall, my mind flooded with all sorts of thoughts. I felt very confident that I could walk down those steps successfully; my concern was making it back up. I pondered the thought, "If I go down all those steps, could I really make it back up without any assistance?" I remembered the many times I had challenges with just a few steps, let alone, "500."

Discussion ensued amongst some of us regarding various concerns as to whether we could make it up or down the steps. When out the blue, the only male in our group, our photographer, began to encourage us, saying things like, "Don't worry, you can do it!" His words penetrated deep to my core, as to put me in check. Oh, how soon we forget! Remember the enlightened, transformed, and electrified experience I'd just had previously, the one that left me feeling invigorated and feeling like I could conquer the world?

Well, what happened, in less than two hours later, to my perspective? I would say I had an Elijah moment, when he had the big demonstration of the power of his God -vs- Baal, and he defeated and killed 400 prophets of Baal. Immediately after the demonstration of God's mighty power, he found himself hiding and wishing for death in fear of Jezebel, who sought his life. Umm, that caught my attention and got me to thinking. How can one go from such a high place to a low in so little time? That's another subject for another book, as God is speaking to me concerning it, but for now, we just need to know that I was immediately brought back to that place of feeling like I could conquer the world again.

Upon arriving at the waterfall, some of my sisters began changing into their bathing suits because they were planning to go to the base of the waterfall. Well, I didn't bring a change of clothes as my late arrival didn't allow me to get the memo, but I was determined not to let that be a determining factor for me. As we entered the viewing area of the waterfall, seeing the beauty of it upfront and personal, I knew I couldn't get this close and not go down to the base, so I joined in with those who were going down.

When I got to the bottom and saw the graceful, sparkling, spectacular scenic flow of water coming out of the earth, it was too exhilarating for me to be that close and not get in. So, I asked the person in charge if I could get in the water with my clothes on. I was granted permission, so I commenced climbing the rocks to enter the water.

Oh my God! What an awesome feeling to be in that water, and what a majestic view, looking up at the water flowing out of the rocks. Again, I felt such a sense of freedom! I don't have the words to describe adequately what I was experiencing. The water was so invigorating that we spent more time than planned in it, and the time had come for us to make the trip back up the steps.

Well, now I was soaking wet, I didn't think about the journey back up the steps before deciding to get in with all my clothes on, but the experience was so awesome it was well worth it. I had no choice but to walk back up those steps wringing soaking wet. My sister "Vee" whom I had just met, stayed back with me along with the tour guide and his understudy.

I was the last one to get to the top, but it turned out to be a real joy, as I had the opportunity to share with them my testimony of how I had been down so long due to medical issues. "Vee" decided to pause and record my testimony, which I have shared in the earlier chapters of this book. Then at another resting point in my journey back up, our tour guide shared a heartfelt story of a friend of his who was in a motorcycle accident wherein a truck hit him, in his fight to return to normal, how he walked those very steps.

It truly was an amazing journey back to the top of the stairs, and to my surprise, it was more challenging to go down the steps than it was for me to climb back up soaking wet. That alone was very interesting. As I arrived at the top, my sisterhood was waiting and began celebrating with me.

It was awesome! We then boarded the bus to return to our rooms to get dressed for our group dinner, so that we could gather afterward to do a recap of our day together.

⧉

We arrived back at our starting point, and I was instructed to go into the visitor's tour office and inform them I was a late arrival. Sister Wyevetra agreed to accompany me there, and upon informing them, I was told, "That will be $129." You could imagine my expression, as I didn't have any money, you read the testimony of how I got to go on this trip. But thank God, who always has our backs! Sister Wyevetra, whom I had just met, said, "I will pay for it!" WOW, another incredible example of unusual and uncommon favor from God! "Won't He Do It… YES HE WILL!"

Now, this reminds me of another important point. How many of you would have decided not to go on this trip alone without any spending money? I myself, if I had been walking in the natural and not by faith, would have never taken this trip alone, especially without any spending money, as we were taught as young people to never go anywhere without what our parents called "emergency money."

And if I were operating from that place of knowing, I would have missed an opportunity to experience what I've shared in this chapter and the chapter before, and you cannot put a price tag on that experience. This also proves that you are in a different frame of mind (thinking) when walking by faith from that of walking in the natural. We must learn how to walk by faith, and not by sight as the True and Living God has a track record we can trust!

***

Finally, we were all dressed and met to eat dinner together, and we had dinner at the same open-air restaurant we had eaten breakfast earlier. You remember how elegant that restaurant was, and the dinner was even more delicious than breakfast.

We had great fellowship with one another as we enjoyed our meal together. We hurried over to the location of our meeting room for the recap of our fabulous day together. This area was all so breathtaking as there was a lot of open space outside; it was beautifully landscaped with extremely colorful plants and vegetation. There was a running stream adjacent, creating a very calming atmosphere.

We all settled down and remained seated as we discussed all the events of the day. Our wonderful Host, Melissa Edwards Brown, did an excellent job facilitating the discussion. She went around the table and allowed everyone to share their experience of the day. There were twelve of us, and it was interesting to hear what each person received.

The consensus was that we all found ourselves challenged in very different ways from crossing the suspension bridges, hiking the Rainforest, to walking a thousand steps (500 down and back up). It was amazing to see how we were able to relate some of the event challenges of the day in direct correlation with how we were or were not showing up to the challenges of our personal lives.

The next morning, we met in the same space for the final workshop. The facilitator played a lesson tape taught by Dr. Miles Munroe entitled, "Activate Your Greatness," wherein he explains we were not a mistake, we are not a biological accident, nor a cultural nuisance, but that we came to this earth with a purpose. This was a powerful session as it caused us to delve deep into discovering the purpose for which we are here.

She expounded on the fact that because we came here with a purpose to fulfill a need in the earth, we are a gift. She went on to emphasize we are not a servant to the people we serve; we are to be a servant to the gift, noting if we manage the gift, the people will be taken care of. This was one of my Aha moments that caused some deep thought. It was a different perspective for me, as I always felt I was a servant to the people and could look back over my life as a Leader wherein I made decisions based on that mentality, and can now exam the results from a different perspective. I must say, this was another life-altering moment for me.

I was very thankful I was able to catch that much of the workshop, as I had to leave early. My roommate was graciously generous to pay for me to have a full body massage, and the only time I was able to get it done was during this session of our workshop. This was another of those unusual and uncommon favor moments that God said would be happening on this trip. This was my first ever full body massage; and let me tell you if you haven't already treated your wonderful body to this yet, please take note.

The atmosphere was miraculous and certainly to live for. There was an array of plant life, flowers of all colors, streams running through, and it was given in the outdoor setting; plants lined your quarters for privacy. The sounds were really amazing, as you could hear birds chirping, water running, and the natural aroma of the air was indescribable! I was so impressed to see that people had their young children getting massages.

When you enter for your appointment, you are checked-in and escorted to this sacred cozy area wherein you are told to undress and put on a luxurious white robe and slippers. Then they ask you to relax on comfortable recliner chairs until your therapist comes to retrieve you. While in waiting, you are provided a freshly made fruit smoothie of your choice. Upon completion of your massage, you exit to this sacred area wherein you receive a serving of fruits, nuts, and another drink of your choice. Oh my God, it was all so majestic!

Later in the evening, we had our final dinner together. It was a very elegant gathering, as we all were dressed in white, and there was live entertainment. The dining area was very cozy with dim lighting, and the waiters were very attentive to our desires. This was an amazing culmination of our journey together in Costa Rica, the mini Garden of Eden, as I heard God refer to it.

SELF-REFLECTION

- What did you think about being considered a gift and not a servant to people?

- Share your overall thoughts and feelings about this chapter.

- What dreams have you not yet fulfilled? What are you going to do now to assist in their manifestation?

Chapter 7

THE GREATER WORKS

The number seven symbolizes completion, and this chapter represents the completion of the illnesses and misfortunes I suffered. It marks the end of the old era of my life, one of lack, pain, and struggle. I am truly grateful to find myself at this place, and as you can only imagine, I am extremely thankful to have survived all that I have to enter into my new life and what it has to offer in my new era.

The joy I feel there are no words to describe; it is unspeakable joy. The peace in my life is the kind that surpasses all understanding. The love I feel is certainly beyond this world. I realize I am not just chosen but sent as a Gift to shift the trajectory of my lineage and that of the world. In order to accomplish this task, I will have to totally depend on help from all of my divine sources beyond this realm, and I will continue to expect assistance from them all. "Won't He Do It... YES HE WILL!"

I am expecting everything I need to accomplish my purpose on earth to show up for me daily. The mere writing of this book has so solidified in me the confidence to do whatever is required of me to fulfill my divine purpose for entering this realm. I realize a million-mile journey begins with one step, and this represents me taking my first step. The good news for me is realizing, after looking back over my life, I do not have to fulfill my purpose alone.

I can trust the Living God and His entire Angelic Host, who has brought me this far to continue leading, guiding, and protecting me. I am looking forward to connecting with those whom I have not yet met who are a part of my journey of shifting the trajectories assigned to me. I know there are Divine Covenant Connections I've yet to meet who will be extremely instrumental in this dimension of my faith walk here on earth, and I welcome them all.

⸙

Now that I have left my old paradigm of "Becoming" and have now entered my new paradigm of "Being," all that I am shall manifest from within me. The hardest thing to accept in looking back over my life was realizing my journey was simply to introduce me to the power within.

This is a sad commentary, as one should not have to be fully grown to learn of the power within them, nor should they have to go through hell to discover it. It is something that should be taught to us at an early age; instead, we are taught from birth to search outside ourselves for everything. Never are we shown to search within, where the true power lies. We are told the Kingdom of God is within, yes, but no one was teaching us exactly what it meant or what it encompassed nor how to access it!

My journey has taught me everything I need lies within me, and this is a powerful revelation to awaken to, as we spend a lifetime searching outside of ourselves for what we think we need to be successful in this life. Yet, the paths we take lead us all around, up, and down only to find out there was a straight and narrow path to our divine destiny.

We spend years building what we believe will make us happy, only to find out the real treasure of life is within. From the time we enter the earth realm, we are constantly taught how to use our five senses. At birth, tests are performed on us to make sure our five senses are working, and from there, we are taught to rely on them. Never are we taught about our sixth sense, the third eye we have, even though from birth, we are operating from that sense, and yet no one acknowledges it nor encourages us to strengthen it.

As we stare off into space, smiling and laughing, certainly indicating we see something beyond this realm as infants, we are immediately encouraged to bring our attention to something in the natural, i.e., a parent, toy, or a certain sound, etc. thereby, neglecting to give attention to our sixth sense, and thus begins the process of dimming our inner light and power.

<hr />

We are conceived inside the dark tunnel of a woman where we would spend our time growing and developing the suit we would wear for the entire time of our journey on earth. In this very unique place within the woman (The Womb); everything we need to allow this suit to develop is provided for us, and everything we need to fulfill the purpose for which we would be entering the earth realm is likewise inscribed in us, but we are not made aware of the power and purpose of it.

Once our process of transferring into the human suit is complete, we move from spending this valuable time of transforming from the Spiritual Beings we are, at that point, into the Human Beings needed for earth's assignment, the Gift, to begin our journey traveling down this tunnel, exiting that wonderful place of development to enter this finite space of time.

Entering the earth realm is a very traumatic experience and initiation into our earthly life, which is very different from our humble beginnings. During the entire process from conception to development, we are shielded within a comfortable place of darkness, where we incubate until the scheduled time to make our grand entry into earth.

Immediately upon entering this realm, we experience shock and trauma as we travel from a dark and secure, warm and cuddly place wherein we have been living comfortably in amniotic fluid, to an atmosphere wherein we must immediately adjust to a new element, taking in air, overtaken with bright lights and cold temperatures to the rough way we are handled physically upon entry. I wonder how many of us have thought about how traumatic this process must be to the babies entering this realm and what lasting effects it has on us.

Our true journey begins long before we enter the earth realm; it starts as we are only thought in the mind of our Creator, who looks zillions of years into the future and sees a need for which He calls us forth, as the answer at a particular time to be conceived at a point that would land us in this earth realm at the exact time to go through our process of earth life to position us at the place of need in this realm, equipped with everything needed to fulfill that need which is our God-given purpose for entering planet earth.

The recipients, parents, not recognizing what each Being has traveled through to get here nor understanding their divine purpose, simply acknowledge their arrival and proceeds with their limited plans for this God-ordained unlimited Soul.

"It is time to step out on the water into the deep, I have so much I am revealing," says the Lord. With that being said, and without going too deep into what God is revealing to me, I will attest that God is revealing a lot of things right now that are truly spinning my head because it is so contrary to what I have been taught. So, I am warning you the time has arrived to thoroughly examine what you have been taught, and open yourselves up to allow truth in.

Remember, you cannot pour new wine into old wineskins, or it will burst; and you can't pour anything else into a container that is already full, so be prepared to empty out by unpacking what you've learned to unlearn what you have been taught thus far in this life. There is so much I would like to share that I am not at liberty to at this time.

I will say, we have entered the dispensation of time of

the "Greater Works," which will be done through you and I. We shall experience the fulfillment of prophesy like never before, and that includes the personal ones spoken over your lives, which you have forgotten because it has been so long to fulfilment. I am so happy to be a part of what God is doing in the earth today.

I see so much, this time we live in is all about the Kingdom of God on earth. Yes, the Kingdom of God suffers violence, but the Chosen of God shall take it by force. Those who understand the depth of spiritual warfare and know the angelic army that has been assigned to you, hear the clarion call and rise up you mighty Nation.

Yes, there is great calamity ahead, but it is no different from any other Era in time, wherein there was a changing of the guards, and a transference of wealth. Whether it was in ancient times or only a few centuries ago, there was always chosen people who survived and prospered through it. People of God, this is a time of great destruction, but I decree and declare it is a time when God's chosen people will reign, His true chosen people! We must discern the times and not allow others to discern it for us, and more importantly, we must know who we are and who we represent through this process.

❧❀❧

My God is doing a New Thing, it is springing forth, and I see it. I am very aware of it! He is making ways out of no way; He is making a way of escape for you, a road in your wilderness to get you to His place of fulfillment. He is causing water to flow in your desert to bring you into His overflow. People of God don't be fooled in this time of God's revealing. Gone are the days, wherein those who stole our identity, reaped our harvest, and lived the life God promised us, are going to be able to lie to us anymore! No longer will we sit idly by and allow our enemies to enjoy our inheritance, our promise. Thy Kingdom has come!

During the time of writing this book, Judgement is being executed, and plagues have been released yet again upon this earth. There is great civil unrest in our country and the world. Leadership is divided, chaos is breaking out everywhere, and people are beginning to lose hope, wondering what to do, and how to survive it all.

While God, in His infinite wisdom, has me to release this book entitled, "Won't He Do It... YES HE WILL!" to remind the masses that He is alive and well and expecting His people to repent, return to Him, and surrender their will for His. This book is a living testament of the wonder-working power of God and serves as a reminder that He is the same yesterday, today, and forevermore, and NOTHING is too hard for Him. God will use me to remind the world and encourage His people to gain a Godly perspective of these times in which we live.

We must understand while judgment is being executed, God's Kingdom on earth is rising simultaneously. This earth is the Lord's and the fullness thereof, and what we are witnessing is the reclaiming of God's earth, and the changing of the guards along with the transference of wealth that hereto now has only been seen as God's promise to a people. His Chosen people are ready to manage what rightfully belongs to them; therefore, it all is being returned to us now, voluntarily, or involuntarily.

People of God, we have now entered in! God is calling all those, who have been hidden in caves for years, to come forth, THIS – IS – YOUR – HOUR! The last shall be first, and the first shall be last. It is time for the true children of God (His Chosen) to celebrate, as the dawning of the new day has arrived. I am excited to know that I am a written epistle, being read of men, and I have yielded to the perfect will of God to manifest His divine purpose through me.

I want to encourage everyone to take their focus off the chaos surrounding them and turn your attention to the true and living God within for direction and perspective. This is a great time we are living in, do not miss this awesome time paying attention to all the distractions surrounding you and do not miss your "NEW DAY" preparing for tomorrow.

I want to encourage those who have experienced the loss of loved ones to go through your grieving process but allow the true and living God to heal you and show you how to move on into your divine destiny because God doesn't want anyone to be lost. God is on His throne alive and well, avenging injustices on earth as evidenced through the discernment of events in communion with Him. We must know this by faith, He is a JUST God!

The manifestation of the "Greater Works" requires us, the chosen children of God, to walk in the power and authority He invested in us, as we are not our own; we have been bought with a price. It requires us to be our authentic selves unleashing power everywhere we go to change environments and possess territories God has given us. We must know that a thousand may fall at our side and ten thousand at our right hand, but NONE shall come near us because of the power at work in us, that of the true and living God.

The first part of the "Greater Works" is awakening to the power within, knowing it is for the purpose of bringing you into who you were designed to be so that you will impact this world in a mighty way. We are not here to be enslaved, misused, and abused and left to die! We have a role in making this world a better place for all to enjoy; things are out of order because we, the chosen children of God, have neglected to take our rightful places in society, leaving to others to take care of what God has given us charge over. Now that we have come full circle, it is time to step fearlessly into our rightful places in this universe.

<hr />

As we are ushered into this new dimension of life, it is all about the Greater Works. Jesus said, *"Truly, truly, I say to you, he who believes in me shall do the works which I do; and even greater than these things he shall do"* (John 14:12). What a powerful statement. What could we possibly do that would be greater than what He did as He walked this earth?

Well, here is where I will share some of what God revealed to me on this subject. Without going into much depth, we all pretty much know some of the feats Jesus accomplished during His time on earth, we call miracles, such as; He raised the dead, opened blind eyes, and fed thousands with three fish and two loaves of bread with baskets of left overs, just to mention a few.

One would ask, as did I, "What could be done greater than that?" God began to reveal to me, first and foremost, there is nothing new under the sun. While many will recite that which comes from the sacred scriptures, but very few believe or understand it. As the cycles of life move from one era to another on planet earth, many things change from one-time period to the other, and in that transition, information is either lost and or hidden, thereby making each era seemingly to stand alone in its creation of things.

However, the truth to the statement is what appears in one era of time, while new to that era, does not mean it has not existed before in a previous era. **Case-in-Point:** How do we have buildings and structures existing on earth from earlier eras that we cannot explain how they came into being, i.e., Ancient Pyramids, the lost city of the Incas, etc., which existed thousands of years before Jesus entered the earth, and yet we depict Jesus' era as a time of underdevelopment, and we come into the current era and say this technology is advanced. I'll wait... just some food for thought! Truth is, it is all for the purpose of manipulation and control of the minds of the people. Truth has always been hidden from the masses, but we have entered the era where all truth crushed to the ground is rising and made available for all to see, and in each era, there has always been a revealing of things to come. It was no different in Jesus' era or now.

Just imagine if Jesus lived in a time when there were Billions of people on the planet in a Nation wherein 90% of households had computers? And of that 90%, 92% has access to the World Wide Web (Internet) or if one of every two people possessed a mobile device which gave them the same access to the Internet as does computers? Or if He could log onto a site and have immediate access to a billion people (Face book) or create an account that would put Him in a conversation involving 330 million people (Twitter) or 100 million people (Instagram). Yet, this is the era we live in, which affords us the luxury of such technological advancements.

Jesus used what He had to fulfill His purpose and mandated us to do the same. Given we have so much more available to us to assist in our efforts to advance the Kingdom, which is (*the Greater Works*), we shouldn't have any problems. The scripture tells us in Luke 12:48, to whom much is given, much is required. So, with the advancement of technology and all its capabilities, we certainly are required to perform and manifest much more than Jesus did.

God incarnate, in flesh as Jesus, lets us know that He had the ability to see into the future. Scripture recites times Jesus knew what was going to happen before it happened. Jesus foreknew the technological advancement of mankind was returning and hence charged us with an agenda of greater works by saying, *"Marvel not at the things I do for even greater works shall you do."* The greater works would be the advancement of the Kingdom in the twinkling of an eye.

I would venture to say by utilizing the advanced technology of today, we are able to reach many more people in a fraction of the time it took Jesus to reach the multitudes in His day, which will allow us to be able to transform and reconcile the world back to God exponentially. Remember, the same God, Power, and Anointing are available to us that was also available to Jesus, and it is not limited by time nor space; hence, the exposure for greater use through the utilization of advanced technology.

In 2008, Americans elected the first black President in a country that previously had over 400 hundred years of slavery of the black man, woman, and child. The advancement of technology played a significant role in causing this to happen. Candidate Obama was successful in utilizing the Internet to organize his supporters; prior to the use of the Internet in this manner, it would have taken thousands of volunteers, as well as thousands of paid organizers, and much more time than it took to produce the winning results Candidate Obama manifested. His use of YouTube for FREE advertising was brilliant in getting his message out. This victory is not to be taken lightly. This happened in a country considered one of the World's Superpowers, who is extremely prejudiced against the black man, woman, and child, as evidenced today with the killing of so many unarmed black men in the streets of our cities, and the overpopulated prison system with people of color, just to mention a few pieces of evidence.

Utilizing advanced technology, Candidate Obama won every caucus state required for presidential victory. It was said by Ms. Arianna Huffington, Editor-in-Chief of the Huffington Post at the time, "Were it not for the Internet, Barack Obama would not be President. Were it not for the Internet, Barack Obama would not have been the nominee." This is proof positive of what can be done using advanced technology correctly. This represents the perfect example of how the Kingdom of God can and will be advanced when we utilize the advancement of technology in ways to assure such results, as did Candidate Obama.

Jesus, in His infinite wisdom, knew what tools we would have available to us for use in advancing the Kingdom and therefore issued the mandate. Please note we can do it… We must do it! Jesus had everything He needed to accomplish His assignment, and likewise, we have everything we need to manifest the "Greater Works!"

We must simply awaken to the truth that we, the Chosen, have been tricked into looking at others as the Chosen of God. Therefore, we must denounce the lie and brainwashing to recognize who we really are and whose we are. We must awaken from the spell over our lives to recognize our Creator and the commission upon our lives. As we awaken to the truth, we will recognize our Creator and stop denying His acts to rescue us from destruction and allow ourselves to be elevated into our proper positions in this universe, as the true Chosen Children of the Most High God.

❧～❦～❧

There is a technology springing forth that will change this world as we know it, and we have sat idly by and allowed it to be formed without any say in its implementation. We have not prepared the masses for its impact. This technology is known as "A.I." Artificial Intelligence. We will have to contend with its advancement, and the masses of people have no clue to what is before them in the form of Artificial Intelligence.

The Church is behind the times in its knowledge of the evolution of Artificial Intelligence. A.I. is changing the world and our lives as we know it. The future will be completely different because of our advances with "A.I.," and left unchecked, this world will be run by it and destroyed. But God, and His true Chosen!

Actually, we are behind the eight ball, in our knowledge of the role "A.I." will and is playing in our lives already. We have not yet realized the current jobs – positions that are being eliminated by A.I. We are fast losing many positions to this Artificial Intelligence that people made a living from to support and raise their families. We have not realized the effects this is having on our communities and the world.

We must be mindful there will indeed be a whole lot

140

more changes as "A.I." takes front seat in our lives. But please be aware this Intelligence is as it is named, "Artificial," and will never be greater than its originator, the source from which it comes, "The I Am," which is the Infinite Intelligence "I.I." I cannot stress this enough; please note, "A.I." is out of this world intelligence, but will never, ever, ever be greater than Infinite Intelligence, "I.I.," which is its source!

Mankind's problem is their desire to be greater than their Creator. Mankind has not learned it is not possible for the created to be greater than the Creator. We must return to genuinely honoring the Creator, who is certainly worthy of honor and respect for all that has been given us! It is time to return to the Sacred Order of things, not the "Secret" orders we have come to worship and idolize, but the source of those very orders, the I Am. "The Created will never be greater than the Creator." The sooner mankind learns this, the quicker we will bring harmony back to our earth and our great universe.

Infinite Intelligence has always been at work in our universe; that's how thoughts are able to become things. We have not paid much attention to it before now. It is now manifesting at a tremendous pace, causing us to have to take notice. Will Smith's "iRobot" movie was right on in bringing this information to the forefront. I do not want anyone to be afraid, but you must become aware of what the future is going to look like at the speed in which "A.I." is moving, and that movie depicts it best.

I want you to know mankind's plans will never outlast or win against the Creator's divine plan, although it could be very intimidating and frightening. This is one of the reasons it's recorded in scripture that God repented ever making man in Genesis 6:6 because He knew He had created us with great power and abilities, if not properly managed, would get out of control (A.I.).

The hearts of mankind were desperately wicked and disobedient then, as it is today, set on a course to do whatever they are big and bad enough to do without respect or concerns for the consequences their actions set in motion. As demonstrated with the building of the Tower of Babel in the same chapter of scripture. The people decided they would build a Tower to Heaven. He had to intervene by dividing their language so they could no longer understand one another to stop their plans.

The hearts of mankind can be so desperately wicked that the founding fathers of the United States of America were moved to write in the Declaration of Independence, "... all experience hath shewn that mankind are more disposed to suffer, while evils are sufferable than to right themselves by abolishing the forms to which they are accustomed..." being played out daily not only in America, but throughout the world.

Infinite Intelligence has always been in operation, but for most of us, we have ignored it and simply not obeyed its promptings and directions to us. If you but look at the events described throughout this Testament, you will be able

142

to identify this Intelligence at work.

I promise you there is nothing new as the scripture reveals in the book of Ecclesiastes, it is only new to those who are unaware. True Believers must now become very acquainted with this Intelligence as the Chosen will have to use it to perform the Greater Works and usher in God's Kingdom. The Greater Works must begin with us individually fulfilling the purpose for which we entered this earth, and unfortunately, too many of us do not have a clue as to why we are here.

I, myself, did not discover who I was or my purpose until after having a visitation from God informing me that before He formed me in the womb, He knew me; and before I was born, He sanctified me and ordained me a Prophet to the Nations. Then He said, His words have He put in my mouth. I didn't really understand it for most of my life because no human being, who was responsible for my development, identified it. So, I did not get any specific teachings early on, and I believe that was by Divine Design.

I believe that was God's way of making sure I was not contaminated and therefore, free to be used by Him in unorthodox ways! He will reveal who we are to us when we are ready, with or without Man. I am called to be a midwife to help people, particularly women, identify, unlock, and unleash their divine purpose.

I never knew who I was nor the power of my calling until fairly recent. After working through the Traumas of the last five years of my life, revelations were revealed and made clear. Now, who I am, and all I am called to do, is flowing into my life exponentially. I am experiencing such an acceleration of my identity, and I believe it has to do with me being available and willing to receive it.

God is so good, He understands how we so often feel like we are ready for the divine things of our lives, but in actuality, we are not in most cases, and He keeps and protects us through our process. My experiences have shown me the importance of divine timing. As I look at my life, I now realize how some things, if known earlier, could have frightened me away from my divine purpose.

※～∽∾※

I've had several prophesies spoken over my life only to have 20+ years go by, and I not see their fulfillment. But now, as I gain knowledge and wisdom from on High, I realize I wasn't ready, and all of these years have been preparing me for their fulfillment.

"Won't He Do It... YES HE WILL!" is our reminder of the power at work on our behalf on a daily basis. As we move forward on assignment to regain control of God's planet, we must recognize our individual roles in making this happen. Enough is Enough, we have watched long enough. It is time we use our God-given power to effect change on this earth! I will represent my God the more by speaking truth to power and encouraging people who are called to occupy governmental offices, to come forth in power to establish the government that is upon their shoulders – God's government on earth. This will not be business as usual; it is time for the takeover; we are the chosen ones.

As I realize we are blessed to be a blessing, and it does not just mean material wealth, but that we are chosen and empowered to rule and reign, I intend to spread it around like wildfires! Creation is mourning and groaning for the manifestation of the true sons of God! We are the true sons of God, and the time has come for us to rise collectively in power and authority to rule and reign according to God's plan for our lives and His earth. Will the rightful rulers, the true Chosen of God, stand up and come forth? The clarion call has been released, and we shall see the manifested results!

Our God is Real! Unlike the wizard of Oz, our God is alive and well on His throne orchestrating the rise of His Kingdom on this earth, so ready or not, the Kingdom of the Living God is rising; in the midst of all the chaos, God's Kingdom is rising! We must realize as we have been experiencing God's power on a personal level, we are about to see His mighty move on a universal level on this earth. God is not mocked; there is about to be a grand showdown of the power of the true and living God against the wickedness running rampant on His earth.

We must do as Elijah did with the prophets of Baal and allow the true and living God to demonstrate His power through us. We must do as David did to Goliath; we must confront whatever giants are occupying territory that God has given to us. Both Elijah and David did not back down from those uncircumcised leaders of their day, and we must likewise not be afraid of those who stole our identity and are illegally reigning over God's property today for the earth is the Lord's.

God's grace and favor upon our lives are not just for us to display material stuff and titles; it is there, first and foremost, for us to be empowered to regain control and the managing of God's property, earth, at all cost. We are Ambassadors of the true and living God, His government is upon our shoulders, and the time has arrived for us to bring it forth. We must stand boldly, and command order be restored on the earth, knowing that while weapons are formed, NONE will succeed against us.

It is time we allow ourselves to be used in the fulfillment of scripture today, as our God is the same yesterday, today, and forevermore. So, what He did for Elijah, David, and the rest of His servants throughout scripture, He will do for us in our stand for the rise of His Kingdom.

People of God, it is time we through off the shackles of bondage that have held us back from operating in the Power and Authority Jesus transferred to us in the proper manner, and stop using it against one another in competition. It is time for us to unite and operate in Holy Ghost boldness like never before and rise up and take the land.

If God be for us, who can be against us? If not now, when? If not us, who? Which side are you on? This is why it is vitally important to have a personal relationship with the true and Living God to have the confidence in knowing He is with YOU! People of the Living God, welcome to the Greater Works. This is OUR time!

SELF-REFLECTION

- What connections can you make between greater works and ushering in the Kingdom of God?

- In this chapter I discuss artificial intelligence. After reading, what are your thoughts about A.I.? How should we as the people of God respond to this existence on earth?

• What are your thoughts about the Kingdom of God on earth?

Chapter 8

NEW BEGINNINGS

WOW, I've arrived at the last chapter of the book in the number chapter, which represents new beginnings! I am so overjoyed with the accomplishment of completing this book. As I have shared, God really has been good to me, and now as I enter this time of new beginnings, I welcome all that He has for me in this New Season. When I tell you everything about my life right now is NEW, it is indeed new and exciting!

As I mentioned in the "The Introduction," I realize some didn't make it, but if you are reading this book, you are one of the ones who did, and I'd like to encourage you to know that no matter where you find yourself today, your new beginning is at the end of that journey. The God I serve is no respecter of person, as He demonstrated throughout this book, especially in Chapter 5, when He made-a-way for me to get the money I needed to get my passport and roundtrip plane tickets to Costa Rica within three days. After I heard the testimony of what He had done for another sister, and I aligned my faith for Him to do it for me. What He's done for me and many others, He'll do for you, and greater things will He do for you because He loves YOU!

This is my time of Jubilee! I have come through a lot to get to this place, and I am committed to flying higher and higher and higher where the air is thinner, and I can see clearer. I recognize there is no ceiling to where I want to go or what I want to do, and I will not place any on it. I see everything from a different angle today, thanks to my process. I know I have an unending reservoir of life flowing within me that will keep me going for as long as I need it. My vision is clear, and my expectations are Great! I know there is no good thing my God will withhold from me; I also recognize I am not alone; there is a spiritual army with me daily. I am such a different person today because of all I've been through, and I would say to the world, I wouldn't trade it for anything.

Please know the relationship I have with God is available to whoever will surrender their will and avail themselves to Him, the I Am – the All-Wise, Infinite Source. All you have to do is acknowledge your need for Him, confess your faults, repent and ask to be forgiven, confess Jesus as the Son of the Living God, not the religious Jesus the world was given, but the true risen Jesus, The Christ. Ask Him to come into your life and be the driver, and He will honor your request, and you will enter into your new and redeemed life! Hallelujah! "Won't He Do It... YES HE WILL"

<hr />

I am so full of joy, and I know this joy I have the world didn't give to me, and the world can't take it away! While I have my personal aspirations for moving forward, I am clear, and I hear the Lord requiring me to exchange my aspirations for His Divine Will, and I certainly shall obey.

He is showing me glimpses of where He's taking me. This is a time in my life that I must follow Him like never before and I intend to do just that so when you hear me talking about all my plans just know I am aware at the beginning of each day I must always say "Not my carnal Will, but Your Will be done" I say it that way because I've come to realize my Will today is God's Will, but I do understand as you can see in this book there are times my carnal desires try to creep in to overtake me.

I have entered my New Beginnings, wherein I am reaping the promises God made my forefathers! I am among the Chosen of God, the people whom He formed for Himself, and I shall continuously make known His praise! Hallelujah; I cannot say it enough, this is an awesome time we're living in, and I was created and brought forth for such a time as this in God's Kingdom!

My heart is rejoicing, and I will be my authentic self, honoring the God who chose me in all I do for great is His faithfulness and His ways past finding out. I love my God, and I am committed to being unapologetically me, at all times for "GREAT" is His faithfulness to me!

Now, as I move forward on this journey, I shall fulfill God's mandate on my life, and nothing will stop it. If you have not discovered your divine purpose, I strongly recommend you seek God to reveal it to you. Declare today, "This will be your last day of being alive and not knowing your purpose for being." I am blessed to be a blessing! All things are made new for me now, and I shall continue to show forth His Glory! I am so excited!

I now know the depth of who my God is, and no one can take that from me. God is Love! This is why Love has been so misunderstood in our world because we have not known the True and Living God. Love is a powerful energetic life force infinite and unbound; it is everywhere at all times. It is what our awesome, amazing, majestic, spectacular universe is made of; it's ever-present, flowing freely, unhindered by anything. Love is incorruptible, indestructible, indissoluble, imperishable, and uncontaminated! Love is... Unfortunately, mankind tends to associate Love with feelings, emotions, all things finite, thereby totally missing what Love truly is - God!

In this new elevated dimension of my new beginnings, I shall show forth Love and respect amazingly! Love is not what has been displayed in our world, so I will avail myself as an instrument of Love, a powerful force to be manifested in the flesh.

This is another reason I know I will marry and live a life of bliss full of amazing adventure and virtue, as I have awakened to a higher elevation of Love and its wonderful possibilities (Intent). I've come to understand what I have experienced in the past is in no way to be compared to even a fraction of a measure of what Love is, and my past has no negative effect on the Love that's flowing through me now!

I will be an example of Love and respect by demonstrating my respect of others, understanding that we don't have to always agree, but we must always respect one another's opinion and process. Respect is something we all should seek to demonstrate, recognizing we are ALL uniquely different in our design and purpose. Life is truly amazing! I am looking forward with great expectancy to experiencing it in ways I, up until now, have never known with man.

⁕

Well, now that I have finally arrived at this place wherein I understand my purpose, I am free to go forward in the newness of who I am. Understanding I am a gift given to all I encounter with a very clear and divine purpose of Being. It is with great joy I now move into the place of manifesting on purpose.

No longer will I sit idly by and let things happen in my life and the world around me. I know I am here to effect change, and I intend to walk in the power and authority invested in me through the process of the death, burial, and resurrection of my brother Jesus, The Christ. I am now prepared to walk in my divine inheritance.

Arriving at this place in my life has been a process as we all must go through our process, though each is very different, we must all go through. I have looked through my life and released everything that was dead or dying. I purged from the inside out, beginning with my mind, and have evicted all thoughts that represent lack, pain, struggle, and dependency on things of this world.

I shared in previous chapters how God led me to particular courses to take, which helped me tremendously with this process. Once I renewed my mind, I realized I had heart issues, so I entered my heart and released all negative feelings of hurt, brokenness, and rejection through the process of pensive melancholy.

After clearing the restrictions and blockages of the decaying residue from past hurts, pains, and disappointments in my life, like flit, I traveled to my womb and released all the poisons from life's journey that I had allowed to incubate in that Sacred and Holy place (the inner court) of my womb where all life emerges.

I began excavating my womb to rid myself of all the dead things in life, trying to remain attached to me in order to regain access to that reservoir of power buried deep within me. I am now prepared to walk out my truth and my purpose, knowing everything I need that was hidden in plain sight was uncovered by my process, allowing me to see clearly that which was once hidden.

In this season of new beginnings, I shall keep the limits off my God, and continue to flow in Him, knowing He has already ordered my steps. I need only to continue flowing with Him, allowing the manifested results of my continued obedience to shine forth.

All throughout this testament, you can see my steps have been ordered and the powerful manifested results that followed. I will continue to flow in this vein, allowing greater manifestation of the power of my God to be demonstrated through me on this earth. As I indicated in chapter 3, I will do great exploits because of my relationship with my God, so I am certainly expecting greater!

⌘

God in His infinite wisdom has orchestrated my new beginning, as He has every move of my life by recently using one of His earth Angels to nominate me for 2019 Dress for Success Delegate. I must share with you the unfoldment of events surrounding this process. Dress for Success is a non-profit organization, who empowers women to achieve economic independence by providing a network of support, professional attire, and the development tools to help women thrive in work and in life. Dress for Success economically empowers women across the globe. Most people know this organization for its "Suiting" of women, but it does far more than suit women.

As recorded in an earlier chapter, Dress for Success was there for me when I found myself with nothing but the clothes on my back. I won't go into all of that again. I will share with you how God, unbeknownst to me, pressed upon His earth Angel to notify Dress for Success Atlanta to inform them they must not make a decision about the selection of their choice of names to submit as Delegates before hearing my story.

I was not at all aware of what was going on until I was contacted by my local Affiliate and asked to complete the application and have it in by 4:00pm the next day. For some reason, I never got their information. The next day, I was contacted and asked about it. I explained I had not received anything. Upon checking, they discovered a technical issue that prevented it from being sent to me, so they sent it that day, requesting it be completed by 4:00pm.

I was stuck in traffic on my way to church service when I got this news, so I immediately contacted a very dear sister-friend of mine whom I knew I could get to pull the application up and ask me the questions to complete it for me as I was not able to. Well, I called her, and she was not at home, and this was around 3:00pm. She said she was about 10 minutes away from home and agreed to pull it up and contact me. When she got home, she called me to inform me her computer was stalling; it took her computer about 15-20 minutes to load, which was very unusual as she is a businesswoman and uses her computer daily without any problems.

Once her computer loaded and she was able to pull the document up for me, she quickly informed me it required I do a 450 to 500-word essay. At that point, I thought all was lost as I was stuck in Georgia traffic, and it was just no way I could complete the application and get it in before 4:00. I was instructed to contact my Affiliate and inform them of my dilemma, which I did, and to my surprise, they contacted Dress for Success Worldwide to inform them.

They extended my time to get my application in to 9:00am the following morning, the day they were scheduled to make their decision on who would serve as their 2019 Delegates. I was ecstatic as I knew I could get home from church service and complete the application along with the essay and submit it by that time for sure.

As life would have it, the Service went on until very late in the evening, and I didn't get home until after midnight. I sat up and completed them both, and as God would have it, my essay was exactly 500-words without edit. WOW look at God! "Won't He Do It... YES HE WILL!"

I immediately submitted my completed application and went to bed. Later in the day, I began receiving congratulatory emails informing me I had been selected as one of their 2019 Delegates for the Atlanta Affiliate. WOW, this was so amazing as I had no desire to participate in this manner.

This was a perfect example of how God orchestrates our steps. I don't even know how to help you understand how much this was not on my radar of things to do, but it was nevertheless, God's plan for my life at this time. All I could think about was how the road to being selected was an extensive process that took place over a couple of months, and to see how God brought me in at the very last moment before the decision was made and caused me to be selected was truly an honor! Only God... "Won't He Do It... YES HE WILL!"

WOW, this is one of those moments wherein I have to pause to get my emotions in check, and dry my eyes... My God, My God, My God! You know how the question is asked, "Can you look back over your life and point to an event that altered it?" Well, this was one of those events for me; being selected to represent Dress for Success as one of their 2019 Delegates altered my life forever.

As their Delegate, I was to participate in the 2019 Success Summit – LIVE YOUR LEGACY, aboard the Carnival Cruise Ship *Victory* to Nassau, Bahamas! WOW! Yes, they sent me on an all-expense-paid trip with about 100 other Delegates from around the world to share in this experience.

This would be the first time I ever took a cruise, and my first time to the Bahamas, as it was for many of the women who attended from around the world. This was their way of empowering us as up and coming leaders of the 21st Century; and can I tell you it was 1st Class from beginning to end. Oh my God, I won't go into too many details, but each day was filled with power-packed, life-changing workshops, and adventure.

Since I was recommended to participate at the last minute, and it wasn't something I pursued, I honestly didn't know what to expect. While we were kept up-to-date about everything concerning the trip, I still did not know what to expect. I felt like an empty canvas on which God was about to write upon, and I had no idea the imprint God was going to make on me.

I played full out; I was in it to get everything designed for me. I was committed to not leave anything on the table, but to receive all that had been prepared for me. Presenter after Presenter brought forth empowering messages the entire trip, but it wasn't until the very last day, I felt that Presenter was sent there just to pull my destiny from my womb. When I tell you this Presenter breathed life into my soul! I literally wanted to fall over on the floor and just cry my insides out as she was speaking, but instead, I was given a hug by Joi Gordon, CEO of Dress for Success Worldwide, whose shoulders I cried my eyes out on!

The Presenter, who was sent as my angelic deliverer, came in the form of Patricia Russell-McCloud, who taught around the theme "Navigators, not Passengers." When she opened up with, "You're the One that we've been waiting for," I was floored! It immediately cut to my core and became personal, and I really felt like I was the only one in the room that was actually filled with over 100-women. She had my undivided attention.

While we both reside in Georgia, we never met, and as powerful as she is, I never heard of her before this encounter. God took us over international waters to connect us. It was the content, delivery, and anointing of her message that reached down through the marrow of my bones to pull out my destiny! After every point she made that she wanted us to retain, she would sing in a beautiful melody the words, "I Dare YOU! I Double Dare YOU, holding the note for quite a wild before continuing her message to us.

She expounded on things like "A set back is a setup for a comeback." "When you feel you've reached the end of your rope, you have to tie a knot and hold on because you are next in line." "Write a letter about YOU and give it to someone, and ask them to mail it to you four months later." "When you rise and find yourself on the 46th floor, always remember someone is still on the first floor, so send the elevator back down for them." "The importance of going from Success to Significance," and this next one is the icing on the cake for me, "Failure is the condiment that gives success flavor." All I can say is, WOW! "Won't He Do It... YES HE WILL!"

While I always knew I was called to empower women, this experience made it clear and provided the opportunity for me to do so, as it was a requirement as Delegate to create and execute a Community Action Project (CAP). I never felt I was creative, so I was dreading having to do this project, but God set me up pretty as I had no choice but to create and execute a project of my own. All while on the cruise, I had no clue what my project would be, and even after leaving the cruise ship, though I had been tremendously blessed, I had no idea what my project would be.

One morning, during my meditation time, about a week after returning home, I heard the Lord tell me the name of my Community Action Project. He said, **"It will be called, Women of Destiny, Unveiling Purpose,"** and He proceeded to give me all the details about the program and how to execute it.

⌒⌒⌒⌒⌒

With the financial support of Dress for Success Worldwide and a local private business here in Atlanta, SCOPE IT Consulting, LLC, I moved forward putting my project together as instructed. I would like to share some of it with you here, as it was life-altering for me: My project was centered around the Caterpillar, Chrysalis, and Butterfly.

I adopted the image and quote of Michele 'Chaella' Boddie, which states, "To become a butterfly, metamorphosis is necessary. If the caterpillar never went through this process of change, it would never achieve its great destiny and become its most glorious self. We can reach our great destinies by changing what needs to be changed." Hence the birthing of "Women of Destiny, Unveiling Purpose."

The dilemma I found myself faced with was the reality there are so many broken and hurting adults in our communities trying to be husbands, wives, significant others, or simply trying to be adults without recognizing they are in need of healing and or recalibration.

They don't realize the baggage they carry from past relationships, their upbringing, and environments are a composite of who they are showing up as, and directly affects who they are or what they are portraying, good, bad, or indifferent. Unfortunately, this lack of self-awareness is causing havoc in our communities as we all are learning, "Hurt People, hurt people."

Not recognizing they are the sum total of what they were taught, saw, experienced, and learned, whether it was right or wrong. And because they are the adults now with authority to decide what they will or will not do, many aren't willing to take a deep introspection of who they are and what they are doing to learn how what they are doing is impacting others around them, as well as their current communities.

They, therefore, resist change or anything relating to it, believing they are okay. Then they find themselves on what I refer to as the gerbil wheel of life, moving but not getting anywhere, and thereby never discovering the ease and joy of life, never flourishing, and thriving as we were intended to do, have life and have it more abundantly.

So, I have developed a Community Action Project around the Women, as I believe the African proverb, which states, "If you educate a man, you educate an individual, but if you educate a Woman, you educate a Nation." I am on a mission to assist in establishing a New World order here on earth, by assisting women in discovering and launching out into their Divine Purpose.

By creating an environment conducive to assisting women in discovering the power and authority within them that is absolute and showing them by tapping into it, they have the ability to rise above anything. Teaching them how to use it collectively by joining forces with others to establish the Kingdom of God on earth, not by the will of people to see it rise, but through the correct use of the power given them to bring it forth irrespective of what the people want!

Through Women of Destiny, Unveiling Purpose, I am able to facilitate women in raising their consciousness as to who they are and the power they possess by helping them understand and see their lives as the Caterpillar. Allowing them to enter their Chrysalis to go through their process of shedding everything in their lives that doesn't assist them in becoming their best "Selves" to exiting as the beautiful, uniquely designed "Beings" in the earth they were originally created to be, like the Butterflies the caterpillars morph into.

I proceeded to implement the three cycles of the program. This being the *1st Session* of the *1st Cycle,* I like to refer to as Trimester #1: This is the Demolition Cycle wherein we tear down and destroy the fouler ground of the old foundation, which we built our current lives upon. We identify lies we aligned with, concerning who we are, to be released and destroyed. This Cycle is the unlearning and dismantling of the false self-identity!

I was the Presenter for this session, and I gave an overview of the program about how our lives are remarkably similar to that of the caterpillar as we entered this earth realm, fumbling and squirming around, affected by everything we encountered. Then we grew up, and the world became our Chrysalis as the challenges of life came to help us shed any and everything that didn't assist us in being our best selves.

But we had no knowledge of what was happening to us, so we fought against what came to transform us. I explained to them how these gatherings will serve as our Chrysalis, hence, the reason for the rainbow colored streamers covering the entrance into our sessions, symbolizing leaving the caterpillar stage of life and entering our new Chrysalis to become who we were originally designed to be; the beautiful butterfly, free from limitations, able to fly anywhere we desire to make our mark on this world.

I shared the three stages of our Cycles with this being Session 1, Cycle 1- "Demolition," wherein we would dig deep and dredge up all the muck and mire we have pushed deep down within, covering up pains, disappointments, and traumas of our lives for years.

I began this session by explaining the importance of this being a safe haven where we could share whatever we deemed necessary to uncover who we really are. I like to use my life experiences as an ice breaker to make people comfortable enough to open up, so I started by sharing a devastating event in my life that occurred when I was about 3 or 4 years old, and continued until I was around 8 or 9 years old, events I was later able to connect to some of my behaviors as a teenager and adult.

I shared how I was molested by my mother's brother, and how I knew I was that young because I remember the

Elementary school being across the street and wanting to attend and always being told I wasn't old enough. I would awaken out of my sleep at night to him sucking on my nipple (Breast), and it progressed on as I got older.

I went on to share how I just recently, over the last couple of years through my self-care work, discovered how that affected me growing up from me becoming a teen mom at the tender age of 15 to me later meeting and marrying a man who loved the breast, and how I for years would never allow him to enjoy that part of my body until after we had been together for over 20 years and I had done a lot of self-care work.

I truly believe without these types of honest discussions, we will never understand why people are doing the things they do, as most of the time, they don't even understand why they behave as they do. My husband had every right as a married man to have access to my breasts, yet I denied him that for years without understanding why; and we wonder why things in our lives don't work sometimes. I believe there is a reason for everything, we have to be willing to be honest with ourselves, uncover, and deal with it in order to become whole and healed, lacking nothing.

As I allowed myself to be vulnerable and open in this session, allowing my light to shine, I opened the door and gave everyone else in the room permission to do the same. The release was on, the stage was set, and everyone was digging deep, recalling the things in their lives that they had hidden and stuffed deep within the canvas of their Wombs.

This group was ripe and ready to experience the fullness of what our gatherings were intended to do, reveal, and unleash the beautiful butterfly within!

I purchased a large table size puzzle of butterflies to use in our sessions, which I had everyone to gather around. I asked them to take a good look at the puzzle and share what they saw. They shared things like, "Beauty, community, harmony, unity, and pollination," just to name a few. I explained that is exactly how our lives are supposed to look.

I then instructed them to each remove a piece of the puzzle and hold their piece in their hands. I asked them again to take a look at the puzzle and describe what they saw. They said things like, "Incompleteness, division, lack, separation, scarcity...," and the list goes on. I went on to explain that is how our lives look today because we are missing pieces of the puzzle to our lives, and many of us are out of place.

I then instructed them to, one at a time, try to place their piece of the puzzle where they knew it Did-Not belong. After everyone tried, I asked them to describe their experience with trying to fit their piece where it did not belong. They said things like, "It was difficult, tiring, hard, daunting, impossible..." I explained that is what we try to do with our lives daily; we try to fit in where we were never intended to be.

I then instructed everyone to return their piece to its proper place in the puzzle and asked them to describe their experience in doing so, and they said, "easy, fulfilling, free, unhindered…" I went on to explain that is the way our lives were originally intended to be as a community of people with each part supplying the other, so there is no lack.

The moral of this lesson is to point out our rarity; no two of us are the same. We are all uniquely made to be a part of the larger body (World), and perfectly designed to only fit where we belong with ease and joy. I pointed out the fact that there are BILLIONS of people on this planet, and no two have the same fingerprints, not even those who are a part of multiple births.

It was demonstrated that we are far better together than apart; we are uniquely made to fit into specific places! When we learn this fundamental point, we will eliminate envy, jealousy, and all things that divide us. I concluded by going over our questions for this session and discussing them at length. The theme song for this session was "Break the Shell" by India Arie.

❧❧❧❧❧

We were ready, at least we thought we were, to enter the 2nd session of "Demolition." *Session 2 of Cycle 1:* This is when we brought in Andria Crawley from Maryland to facilitate, and boy did she do a job with this session. We utilized technology and streamed her in, and this was before we even knew there would be a pandemic.

People of God; when I tell you, this sister tore open our last session on "Demolition." WOW, you should have been there! My sister Andria Crawley tore into us with the utilization of the excavation process!

This particular session, along with another, got the most raving reviews from participants, and rightfully so because this Presenter did exactly what I was hoping she'd do, and that was to show us how to successfully excavate the depths of our wombs. When I tell you, she did just that by explaining to us how we needed to be sure we utilized the correct tools as we do the work of excavation.

She talked about the tools and their use in excavating and how we each are at different stages of the process of excavating and therefore require different tools. This sister used the illustration of how we are so overloaded and stuck in our mess that we are moving around like the "Walking Dead" using the analogy of Zombies.

Family, you had to be there to get the full effects, OMG! Her title was *"The Burden of Truth,"* talking about how our denial of our situations become burdensome because we don't want to deal with the truth of our lives. She broke it down to how Zombies walk and are controlled by outside forces, noting that so are we, as a result of refusing to deal with the truth of our lives, to how they eat of human flesh, correlating how our denial of the truth of what's really happening in our lives is eating us alive; to them not feeling pain, and how we are going through life numb from the denial of our circumstances!

She went on to share three steps to freedom from such

conditions: 1) Uncovering, 2) Identifying, and 3) Going through our process for elimination. She explained the key is "TOTAL SURRENDER!" My God, My God, My God! It was truly a blessing and what a POWERFUL way to end the sessions on "Demolition!" The theme song for this session was "I Need YOU To Survive" by Hezekiah Walker.

Next we Entered the *1st Session of the 2nd Cycle,* I like to refer to as Trimester #2: This is the Reconstruction Cycle wherein we began to build upon our newly formed foundation, through renewing of the mind and the unveiling of the true self!

Now keep in mind I had to modify this program, which is designed to be a 9-month program; hence, the use of trimesters. I condensed it to 6-months for this Community Action Project because of their timeline. As we quickly entered this 1st Session of the 2nd Cycle, which would have been the 3rd session of the 1st Cycle, "Demolition," in the 9-month program, it was evident this session was critical to the program.

As a result of going so deep in dredging up our deep-rooted stuff, we needed this 3rd session to properly release all that we had dredged up to clear the way in preparation of entering the new Cycle, "Renewing the Mind." So, as we entered this Cycle prematurely in the 6-month project, we now had to spend a considerable amount of time releasing what we all were experiencing as a result of the residue of the Demolition process before moving on to "Renewing the

Mind."

As the Visionary, it was beautiful to see how everyone was expressing the things they were experiencing in their lives since our last session, which was clearly a result of the Demolition process of opening our pandora boxes. While it wasn't pretty, and it was very emotional, we all agreed it was a necessary part of the process to be free.

As we cleared this process, we then proceeded ahead with Session 1 of Cycle 2, "Reconstruction, Renewing the Mind," wherein I was again the Presenter. I opened this session by presenting each of the ladies with a book from our suggested reading list entitled, "The Anatomy of the Spirit" by Caroline Myss, PH.D. The author does an excellent job of breaking down our anatomy and explaining how we possess power and are made up of energy.

I emphasized the importance of our taking in new information to support and sustain our new growth, encouraging everyone to read and study the book as it is truly empowering. I talked extensively about our suggested reading list encouraging the participants to not limit themselves to just that list, but to take the opportunity, now that they had emptied out, to gather new information as they are led, noting they have made room to receive and can now be poured into.

I used this session to prepare them for what was to come in terms of renewing their minds and to get them ready to receive the Presenter, who would be doing the 2nd Session of

Reconstruction, Renewing the Mind. I felt something very powerful was about to happen for our group in that session, and it did. The theme song for this session was "Time to Believe" by Forever Jones.

⚜

2nd Session of 2nd Cycle - "Reconstruction, Renewing the Mind" You never know who's in your mist, which is why the bible tells us in Hebrews 13:2 (KJV) "...to entertain strangers: for thereby some have entertained angels unaware." One of our very own participants was tapped to serve in the capacity of Presenter for this session.

Ms. Star Waters, known as The Wellness Wizard, did a fabulous job, walking us through the conditioning of our minds showing us how we must be in control of our perception of things. She expounded on perception as reality and the importance of understanding that, as we seek to manifest a new life.

She shared that the foods we eat negatively affect our brains, perception, and behavior while altering our DNA. All of which causes us to be susceptible to sicknesses, diseases, and having pre-existing conditions at alarming rates, making us vulnerable to early death through bacteria and virus infections.

Ms. Waters went into deep teachings about the origin of our current diet and the effects it has on who we are by showing portions of the documentary entitled, "The Post

Traumatic Slave Diet," which can be found on YouTube. It was a powerful message showing how we were forced into our current diets through slavery, a diet detrimental to our very existence. She encouraged everyone who has not seen the full documentary to be sure to set some time aside to watch all of it.

She indicated that when God made us, He placed us in the Garden for a reason, noting how our lives most resemble the plant, which is why a plant-based diet is best for our overall health and wellbeing. She went on to share how she creates flower essences to assist individuals in clearing their energy fields and purging their bodies of foreign invaders.

She explained how powerful the use of flower essence is to the body, mind, and spirit, as well as how powerful essential oils are to the healing and maintaining of life, noting both of which come from the plant.

She went on to explain how before slavery, our ancestors lived off the land and were healthy Beings, living long and prosperous lives till Post Slavery, becoming disease-infested, deteriorated, and dying at a young age, impoverished. She shared how food is one of the weapons used to suppress, control, and kill us, explaining how our current diets consist of food-like substances, which are not really food. She showed the group a Sankofa bird, explaining the need for us to go back and fetch the ways of our ancestors before we can move forward to regain our health and vitality.

Ms. Waters also shared how she was able to release a

very large amount of excess weight from her body by changing her diet while simultaneously eliminating diabetes, which she was told could not be cured. She showed before and after pictures, and expressed the importance of aligning our mind, body, and spirit through the foods we eat.

Her session was the other session that got rave reviews, along with actual testimonies from participants of their results, utilizing the techniques she taught in this session. We learned so much you simply had to be there! The Wellness Wizard selected a personal theme song for this session, "Black Butterfly" by Sounds of Blackness, so we had two theme songs. The original theme song was "Powerful" by Jussie Smollett and Alicia Keys.

I gave the ladies an assignment to select one of their AHA moments from any of the sessions that shifted their lives and to be prepared to showcase it in our next session.

<hr />

1ˢᵗ Session of the 3rd and final Cycle, I refer to as Trimester #3, wherein we exercised our confidence in who we have become in what I call the Showcasing Cycle. This Cycle deals with the strengthening of muscles to arise in the newness of becoming Women of Destiny, who took the challenge to join with other sisters on the path to grow from crawling on the ground as caterpillars to soaring like the Beautiful Butterflies they are. These women left their Chrysalis to fly to new heights unknown!

The ladies really brought it in this session. OMG, these ladies were so awesome; they brought to life my ability to measure the results of the program as they took their time to expound on what shifted their trajectory during our gatherings. They really showcased who they had become.

One participant shared it was the demonstration of the puzzle, the uniqueness of each puzzle piece, and how we are each a small piece of a larger puzzle. She went on to explain that it made her look in the mirror to assess where she was trying to fit in this life and whether she was a part of the solution or the problem. The ladies really showed themselves strong! The theme song for this session was "Won't He Do It" by Koryn Hawthorne, Ft. Roshon Fegan.

2nd Session of the 3rd Cycle: Finally, the grand finale of Women of Destiny, Unveiling Purpose. The time of this gathering fell on the cusp of our getting the news about Kobe Bryant and the eight who died in the helicopter crash, so the session had to be delayed by about 2 hours as everyone in the room was affected by the news as it was coming forth. I used this time to allow everyone to vent their emotions before proceeding with our scheduled program.

As we moved on in our program, each woman took their time to express who they have become and where they go from here. One sister announced how she, through the utilization of the techniques taught by Star Waters, manifested her tax Business with clients overflowing. She shared her marketing material with us and expressed how overjoyed she was with her progress since coming to the gatherings.

Again, it was so much, you really had to be there, but I truly hope this summary helps you experience some of what we received. I concluded this session by handing out framed Certificates to each participant along with a gift of three beautiful butterflies they each can display in a location of their choice that would forever remind them of who they have become.

⸎

So, you see, my being selected as Dress for Success 2019 Delegate and participation in Living Your Legacy on the Carnival Cruise Ship Victory to the Bahamas, definitely altered my life and shifted me into my divine purpose.

Expect to hear more about the Women of Destiny, Unveiling Purpose Program, as I will be facilitating it on a regular basis.

If you are looking for an excellent non-profit organization to donate to and receive a tax write-off, I strongly recommend "Dress for Success Worldwide." Likewise, if you ever need IT services, I certainly recommend supporting SCOPE IT Consulting, LLC, as the owner has proven his commitment to putting financial support behind activities that advance the community. You can find their information on the Contact Information page at the end of this book.

I would be remiss, if I didn't ask you to throw your financial support behind Northside Hospital, Dr. Asad Bashey, MD, PhD's Oncology Team. They are the best in the world! Their information can be found on the contact page as well.

In this time of New Beginnings, I am committed to assisting in the manifestation of the Kingdom of God on earth. I will continue to walk in my divine destiny, fulfilling the call on my life to be a midwife, as a Personal Life Coach, helping people unleash into their divine purpose!

Please feel free to reach out to me via my contact information also at the end of the book. "Won't He Do It... YES HE WILL!" It is YOUR time to soar like the eagle you are!

⋘⋙

SELF-REFLECTION

- After experiencing this last chapter, are you now reminded of life-changing moments wherein you were ushered into a new place in your life? Describe it here.

- What can you do to tap into your authentic self?

- Share your overview of this chapter, and what you got from it?

ACCOLADES OF THE AUTHOR

"And now your heroine is standing up for herself too and calling for justice. I am confident that in this leg of your heroine's journey, you get to live a life full only of love, reciprocity, and honesty. You deserve nothing less."

Stefana Serafina
Founder of Intuitive Body and Dance

"This is not about my love for you, Mom; this is me and the book and how it relates to everyone in society. It is PERFECT in touching the hearts of many, as many have sailed on this same boat of life."

Wajutome Goodluck Obriko
Nigeria, Africa

"The Activator, Powerful Woman of God"

Gallio B. L. Gumbs

"The Survivor and Powerful Voice of God"

Cynthia Harper
Founder/CEO of The Cynthia Harper Show

"YAY!! CONGRATS!!! You can manifest earthly law-defying miracles, like nobody's business!!"

Debrena Jackson Gandy

"28 And we know that all things work together for good to them that love God, to them who are the called according to his purpose."

(Romans 8:28)

ABOUT THE AUTHOR

Joyce R. Rogers knew early in life about her calling to assist people in reaching their goals and aspirations, for she has been motivating and encouraging people to dream and pursue their aspirations since elementary school. As the years went by, she was always the one her peers looked to for advice whenever they found themselves up against life's challenges.

It's no surprise that she has grown into a successful Certified Life Coach and dynamic Consultant. Joyce wasn't interested in becoming a Certified Life Coach under just anyone, so she waited until she was divinely led to the Convergence Coach Certification Program, designed to Certify Extraordinary Leaders who are Called to COACH.

Joyce obtained leadership training from Leadership Anne Arundel, Neighborhood Leadership Academy, SCORE, and the PATH program, and received recognition for outstanding Commitment to Personal Development. Joyce's commitment earned her the Achievement Award for Mediation Awareness, as well as the Governor's Citation in appreciation of her outstanding services to the citizens of her hometown of Maryland. She has Chaired and Co-Chaired many Civic Boards and Commissions, and has served on many local, state, and national political campaigns, she has even run for public office against a 20-year incumbent.

Additionally, Joyce is a mother of nine children and currently has twenty-two grandchildren and one great-grandchild with the second expected in December 2020. She is a woman of GREAT substance and has spent more than forty years caring for others only to discover the importance of *Self-Care* in her later years. Since her discovery, Joyce has learned life is not to be balanced, but harmonized. She believes no one should ever give away more of themselves than they are willing to have restored and replenished. Joyce believes in God, Family, and Community, and she is an Ambassador of Christ, Anointed and Appointed to Lead in the 21st Century.

CONTACT INFORMATION

WOMEN OF DESTINY, UNVEILING PURPOSE
Joyce R. Rogers, Author
Coach_Joyce@aol.com
404-919-5045

DRESS FOR SUCCESS WORLDWIDE
32 East 31st Street
New York, New York 10016
212-532-1922

SCOPE IT CONSULTING, LLC
3235 Satelite Blvd, Bldg 400, Suite 300
Duluth, GA 30096
888-SCOPE-27

Asad Bashey, MD, PhD
Blood & Marrow Transplant Group of Georgia
5670 Peachtree Dunwoody Road
Suite 1000
Atlanta, GA 30342
404-459-8510

Made in the USA
Columbia, SC
18 November 2020

24830626R00115